ALL SAINTS
AND ALL SOULS

Sermons by and Remembrances of

Rev. Lee Reid

May the spirit of God surround you, wherever you may go.

William Reid

PETER E. RANDALL PUBLISHER
PORTSMOUTH, NEW HAMPSHIRE
1998

Additional copies available from
    Wallace Reid
    208 King Street
    Englewood, NJ 07631

ISBN 0914339-67-2

Peter E. Randall Publisher
Box 4726, Portsmouth, NH 03802

CONTENTS

SERMONS

All Saints and All Souls

UNITY IN DIVERSITY

The above logo, which is the official symbol of the Unitarian Universalist Congregation of the Palisades, in Englewood, New Jersey, was designed by Rev. Lee reid to emphasize that we are committed to racial and cultural diversity.

We have changed the last part of our name to congregation. Before Lee died, we were named the Unitarian Universalist Society of the Palisades.

The photograph of Rev. Lee Reid on the rear cover of this book is Lee when she was younger, a freckled-faced Irish beauty. Our family felt this picture best expressed the Lee we love, because even then, her countenance was that of a relentless optimist, inviting you to dialogue with her.

Wallace Reid, MSW, MS, CASAC

ACKNOWLEDGMENTS

Permission to publish materials from the following sources is hereby gratefully acknowledged.

Alfred A. Knopf, Inc. for a poem from *Circles On The Water*, a collection of poems by Marge Piercy, copyright 1982 by Marge Piercy.

Bantam, Doubleday and Dell Publishing Group, for a selection from a Doubleday book, *When the Saints Go Marching Out*, by Charles Merrill Smith, copyright 1969 by Charles Merrill Smith.

Dr. F. Forrester Church, Minister at the Unitarian Church of All Souls in New York City, for "As The Wolves See It: Truth and Reality," a selection from his book, *The Seven Deadly Virtues*.

Reverend Holly Elaine Horn, Unitarian Universalist minister at First Unitarian Church in Philadelphia, for the poem "Praise For What Rises."

Liveright Publishing Corporation, 500 Fifth Ave., New York, New York, for the E. E. Cummings poem "i thank You God for most this amazing," from the book *COMPLETE POEMS: 1904-1962* by E.E. Cummings, edited by George J. Firmage.

Carolyn McDade, for the words to the song "Spirit Of Life," copyright 1981 by Carolyn McDade.

Linda Weltner, for an article she wrote for the *Boston Globe*. Linda is a Unitarian Universalist and is author of a book titled *No Place Like Home*.

Dr. John Burton Wolf, Minister Emeritus at All Souls Unitarian Church in Tulsa, Oklahoma, for "A Reminder At Pledge Time."

Hope Publishing Co., Carol Stream, IL, for "Bring Many Names," words by Brian Wren, copyright 1989.

PREFACE

Rev. Lee Reid, an early feminist and anti-racist, increasingly developed the ability to lead and transform people for the better. She helped people become more honest, more caring, more feeling, more thoughtful, and YES, more spiritual. Her deeply moving sermons and ministry invited personal transformation and helped build a strong sense of a loving community in our congregation and with other groups who met with her. Those who knew Lee personally, family and friends, before and during her ministry, had the added benefit of a closer, longer relationship with her. As you might guess, I have made a few changes after being married to Lee for 42 years. OK, maybe more than a few.

Among her many facets, Lee had the three qualities which I believe we all need to foster, in order to help others to transform, to grow, their souls. Emphasized by the therapist Carl Rogers, these may be all that any caring person needs: Empathy, the ability to enter, as well as possible, into the world of another person's feelings and meanings and to sense these as the person does, without evaluating or judging them. Second, unconditional positive regard for the person (not necessarily unconditional love!) And last, the helper's congruence, to be in tune with one's own feelings and meanings.

One definition of a saint is a charitable, unselfish, patient person, worthy of high esteem and living according to a religious system. One definition of a soul is a person considered as an inspiring force - a leader. A saint... and... a soul? Yes, I believe Rev. Lee Reid meets these definitions. The title of this book, *All Saints and All Souls*, is the title of the first sermon in this book. In it, Lee names people who she categorizes as saints. I'm putting Lee at the top of my saints - and souls - list! My three daughters, Sarah, Martha, and Kate usually avoid hubris like the plague. But they do agree with my vote for Lee.

Wallace Reid

The first sentence should read:
Non-priestly religion has long
upheld the spoken word as the
center piece of a weekly service.

ABOUT LEE REID

Non-priestly religion has long been upheld as the centerpiece of a weekly service. In recent years in Unitarian Universalism, the chalice is recognized as the symbol of the open mind and an inclusive heart, yet there is no substitute for the inspiration to be found in a skillfully crafted sermon. Thus is the understanding enriched and the commitment deepened.

Rarely has this non-dogmatic religious art form been more beautifully created or more effectively presented in the weekly discourse delivered by Lee Reid. I knew Lee and Wally when I lived in Westchester County and was Leader of the White Plains Ethical Society. I delivered a sermon at the church on occasion.

Some years later I relocated in Northern New Jersey in order to pursue my career as a psychoanalyst. I was delighted to see that Lee was minister of the new UU Society in Englewood. Having recently retired as an Ethical Culture Leader, I was free to attend her services occasionally and was enchanted by her sermons. I was equally delighted with the transracial make up of the congregation she labored so hard to create. One of the first Lee's sermons that I heard was "As The Wolves See It." Not only did her words set me thinking about those with whom I differ, but her decision to include in the service the recorded music of a wolf pack's nocturnal howl seemed highly appropriate. Shortly thereafter I became a member of Lee's congregation.

Those of us who hold to a more humanistic view of death, as well as those who may hold a more traditional view, all may well appreciate the way in which the essence of a person's life and efforts can live on in the printed word or recorded speech. We are indeed fortunate that after Lee's untimely and tragic death this fine collection of her sermons has been made available.

These spoken essays were labors of love. I now know that she would often sit up most of the night before speaking in order to give her words the form and finishing touches she felt they needed. These words are in a sense Lee Reid.

from Walter Lawton

OBITUARY

Rev. Lee Reid
1932 - 1996

Rev. Lee Reid, Minister of the Unitarian Universalist Society of the Palisades of Englewood, NJ, died on Friday evening, November 22, of injuries suffered in a traffic accident two days earlier. She was on her way to attend a UUSP Board of Trustees meeting when she was struck by an automobile while walking across Piermont Road in Closter, NJ. The accident occurred around 8:40pm in a poorly lit area. She was rushed to Hackensack Hospital by helicopter. Her husband Wally, her daughters Sarah, Martha, Kate, Sarah's husband Larry Braverman, Sarah's daughter Isabel Braverman, and Kate's husband Scott Willis, kept a vigil at the hospital over the next two days. They were joined by many members of the congregation.

Eight Years in Englewood

Lee came to Bergen County, NJ in 1989 to build a Unitarian Universalist (UU) ministry in the ethnically and culturally diverse area encompassing Englewood and surrounding towns. She helped form the UU Society of the Palisades with a handful of residents, and the Society soon began holding its religious services at Flat Rock Brook Nature Center. The Society grew to roughly 70 members under her leadership. Our members regarded her ability to preach on liberal religious values as her greatest strength.

Her activities in the community included active participation in the Bergen County Martin Luther King Birthday Program Committee, helping the Parents of Biracial Children Support Group to get its start, and that organization now includes over 100 families in Bergen County. Lee was instrumental in the formation of the Neighbor to Neighbor Dialog, which allowed Englewood, Leonia, and Tenafly residents to discuss issues of racism and school regionalization. She also instigated re-formation of the Interfaith Clergy group of Englewood, was elected to the Englewood Municipal Committee, and served as county committeewoman for the Democratic Party.

Path of a Unitarian Universalist

Lee was born Laura Lee Morrissey in Buffalo, NY, and raised in a Roman Catholic family. She credited her mother with teaching her about the unfairness of prejudice. Wally relates a story Lee told that one of her mother's acquaintances warned Mrs. Morrissey that her daughter had been playing with a Jewish girl in the neighborhood. Mrs. Morrissey ended her relationship with the acquaintance, and made her daughter understand why.

Lee was a voracious reader in high school and said that her best time during those years was spent in the library listening to T. S. Elliot and Marianne Moore read their poetry on Caedmon records. It would not surprise her friends today that she had an active social life, but we may be surprised to know that she was also a college cheerleader.

Lee obtained her B.S. in art education from SUNY at Buffalo in 1954, and married Wallace Reid in December of the same year.

The Reids were not active members of any church for about six years. They noticed ads in the paper for sermons at the Unitarian Church of Buffalo, which was led by Reverend Paul Carnes, a dynamic minister who later became President of the UUA. In 1961, a friend in their neighborhood who was a member of the church invited them to a service. Lee said she knew when she walked into the church and heard the choir that she had found her spiritual home.

Lee and Wally had two daughters, Sarah and Martha at the time, but Kate soon arrived. All three daughters were dedicated in a single ceremony in the church. Lee became active in religious education programs.

The family was relocated to Westchester Co., NY by Wally's employer, Union Carbide, in 1967. Lee became an art teacher in the Somers, NY school district that year and continued teaching until 1987. Soon after their move, Lee and Wally joined the Unitarian Universalist Fellowship of Northern Westchester in Mount Kisco, NY. Lee again was active in religious education. Later, she served as President of the Mount Kisco Fellowship and then as its lay religious leader from 1983 to 1988.

She felt called to become a minister and enrolled in New York Theological Seminary, in Manhattan, in 1985 at the age of 53. NY Theological Seminary had a diverse student and teacher population. The majority of students were African American or Hispanic, and many denominational affiliations and theological viewpoints were represented among the students. Lee said that she gained a deep appreciation for racial, cultural and religious diversity. She also became convinced that affirming and welcoming diversity could be a central theme for her own ministry and an energizing principle around which to build the ministry of a congregation.

Lee graduated at the top of her class with a Master's of Divinity in 1988 and was rated best in preaching.

Service to Denomination

Lee Reid was heavily involved in denominational affairs. She and Wally were among the four cofounders of UNILEAD, a leadership school for Unitarian Universalist lay persons serving the UU District of Metro NY and also the Joseph Priestly District. She served as co-chair and steering committee member for Life on a Star religious conferences on Star Island, the Unitarian Universalist summer conference center in the Isles of Shoals, New Hampshire. Lee may have perfected her use of the late night conversation as a means of spiritual renewal on Star Island. Past and present UUSP board members knew from board retreats that Lee's desire for conversation peaked well after midnight, but this trait endeared her to her fellow Star Island conferees.

Lee also served on committees for NY Metro Women's Association, the NY Metro UU Ministers' Association, and was a founding member of the Ramapo Mountain UU Ministers' Study Group.

In addition to Wally, her daughters, and granddaughter, Lee is survived by her mother Laura Morrissey and brother James Morrissey. Daughter Sarah is pregnant with her second child. We can also add that she is survived by a grief-stricken congregation, which is resolved to continue her work.

The memorial service was held at Central Unitarian Church, Paramus, NJ on Dec. 15 at 2 pm.

Last Lines

Lee had her Lines from Lee column written out for this newsletter and in the packet of papers she was bringing to the Board of Trustees meeting on Wednesday, Nov. 20. Here is her final message to her congregation:

Well, if I had any doubts before, they are gone. The UUSP is definitely destined for greatness. The Harvest Moon Ball proved that we are a congregation of MOVERS and SHAKERS. The energy and enthusiasm, the grace, the style, the originality, the STAMINA displayed on the dance floor was truly awesome. As we channel all that into the other 364 days of our congregational year, the sky's the limit. So come on, everybody, just keep shaking your booties. We're bound for glory!

A big thanks to visionaries and organizers Richard and Louise Lasota and to everyone who contributed and participated.

And now, onward to the winter Holiday Season. Its a season for fun and friendship, for having and making memories. It can also get pretty hectic; too little time, too many lists. Well, here's yet another one: a to do list for December:

This holiday season, mend a quarrel.
Seek out a forgotten friend.
Dismiss suspicion, and replace it with trust.
Write a love letter.
Share some treasure.

Give a soft answer.
Offer encouragement.
Manifest your loyalty in word and deed.
Keep a promise.
Find the time.
Forgive an enemy.
Listen.
Apologize if you are wrong.
Try to understand.
Flout envy.
Examine your demands on others.
Think first of someone else.
Appreciate.
Be kind; be gentle.
Laugh a little.
Laugh a little more.
Deserve confidence.
Take up arms against malice.
Decry complacency.
Express your gratitude.
Welcome a stranger.
Gladden the heart of a child.
Take pleasure in the beauty and wonder of the earth.
Speak your love.
Speak it again.
Speak it still once again.

Happy Holidays,
Lee

From the Unitarian Universalist Society of the Palisades
Newsletter -December 1996 issue, Al Post, Editor.

REMEMBRANCES OF REV. LEE REID

By Lee's daughters:

Sarah Ellen Reid

My mom always made holidays special and exciting. She developed many family traditions which we faithfully followed each year. Even when we were grown up we still had fun observing these traditions., such as an egg hunt at Easter time. My mom was an expert egg hider and invariably one egg could not be found, and mom would forget where she hid it. Two weeks later, when it started smelling it would be found—usually a green egg hidden among the green leaves of a house plant. I really miss my mom at holiday times, but I am joyful that she gave me traditions that I can carry on with my own family.

Martha Mary Reid

My mother had such an encyclopedic mind and such a sharp memory. I could always call her when something was on the tip of my tongue, a word I couldn't think of, somebody's name, a quote, a vague memory, and she would know what it was. A few years ago, I'd had a recurring dream of a strange place near Niagara Falls that had large man-made rectangular pools of water with violently churning whirlpools. I was sure this was a real place I had visited as a child. I remembered walking on concrete sidewalks around these pools and I remembered that there were some nuns there in full length habits. No one else in the family recalled this, but when I started describing these artificial maelstroms to my mother she responded,

"Yes — and there were nuns there."

It was wonderful to have that corroboration!

As a child, I had such great confidence and pride in my mother's knowledge of nature. On Mother's Day we would pick paper bags full of wild-flowers for her (an ecological sin I shudder to think of now). She would put them in little colored glass vases in the window and tell us the names of all of them. Any insect, leaf or animal I came across, she could tell me its name and something about it. She knew that the little animals living under our back door sill were shrews, not moles, and that they were poisonous. Somebody challenged me on this point once, so I looked it up in the dictionary — some are poisonous. You were right, Mom (of course)! When we moved to Westchester from Buffalo she kept a list of all the birds she saw. One year she spotted a rare appearance of some little birds on their migratory path. I can't remember what they were, maybe redpolls? I wish I could ask her.

I still reach for the phone a lot to call her. Even though I know I can't see her any more, I feel like I should be able to call her, wherever she is. There are so many things I still need to ask her—things that only she can tell me.

Kate Elizabeth Reid

When I was growing up, we lived on 4 acres of woods, complete with a swampy frog pond, teeming with life in all its various forms. I spent many hours alone out there watching frog eggs develop, looking under rocks and examining weird fungi. My mom was an avid bird watcher and naturalist, and taught me to identify many of the plants and birds out there. She loved animals and was always involved in the rescuing of one creature or another: Snakes in the shag rug, flying squirrels on the curtain rod, you name it.

Once, in the dead of winter, my mom discovered a peeper in the bathroom (A frog, that is.) I'll never forget how she loved to tell that story, about finding a tiny , hopping ball of dust, under the radiator, and how she put it in a bucket in the bathtub, until we made a terrarium for it. She named it Prince, and when I got home, she said "There's a Prince in my bathtub!"

She especially got a kick out of how Prince would change himself from brown to bright green, and sing,, but only when I whistled the theme from Love Story. I can still picture her telling that story in her animated way, with that gleam in her eye. I'm sure that anyone who knew her, is picturing her that way right now.

from *Paula Reid*, Lee's niece

My memories of Aunt Lee are that of a very special hand made

Christmas card that my family received from her every year. Now, I have grown-up and have begun my own family traditions. Every December we share in the creation of our hand crafted season's greetings card. Always on my mind is the inspiration I received from Aunt Lee many years ago.

from *Rahda Sukhu*, of New York City, family friend:

Sarah Reid was my classmate at Purchase College. We lived together off campus. Although Sarah always invited me as well as our other friends ("the gang") to enjoy holiday meals with her family, I usually chose to spend the holidays alone. Finally, I accepted. There was no need to "be on your best behavior" nor to "dress to impress." Lee and Wally welcomed us, the gang, as we were. The food was ever plentiful and Lee's cooking was superb. I'll never forget Lee's chili and cornbread, Waldorf salad, and homemade cranberry sauce. Needless to say, I returned many times.

I often thought how lucky Sarah, Martha, and Kate were to have such special parents. They definitely were "cool." Lee and Wally became the honorary parents of the gang. The gang will miss Lee dearly.

Over the years, I shared various residences with Sarah and her husband, Larry. We became very close friends and the entire Reid family became a second family to me. Unfortunately, my family will never meet Lee nor will I have the honor of her performing my marriage (if ever...).

Lee demonstrated that we can make a dream become reality. I always think of her when I feel "it's too late" to achieve my goals. I feel inspired by her strength, conviction and determination that turned her dream of becoming a minister into a successful reality. Initially, I was weakened by her loss. Now, I feel strengthened by the memory of this powerful woman.

Remembrances by those in our community and the friends she had in the broader Unitarian Universalist community

from *Cassandra Jennings-Hall*:

I am profoundly affected by her death, as well as her life. I wondered often how Lee had become so deeply ingrained in my being. How could this be? I've only known this feisty women two years yet when she smiled on me I felt blessed. I felt as though she had the ability to touch my soul. I think I benefited from knowing her and because of her I am back on the path, I am more open and giving of myself and my time. Thank you Lee.

Procrastination is my biggest sin, having had breast cancer, I understand life's limitations and I now live life more fully. But I am a master at procrastination. The instance of Lee's life brought this sin vividly to my face. I have to work at this because now I know that each day of life is a gift that I should use wisely.

Thank you Lee.

from *Cherie Harris:*

You were my life. You were all that I lived for and you guided me down the path of goodness. You were my shimmering star that gave me light, hope, and courage as I faced trials and tribulations, pain and heartache, and even joys and sorrows. Your were the one. The one whom I, myself, as many others did, looked up to as a best friend, as a companion, as a mother, or as someone who they could feel comfortable just talking to. You were the one who brought smiles to frowning faces, the one who soaked up sad tears, the one who was always there.

But things have changed. You're not here anymore with us physically, but you're here emotionally and of course spiritually. You are still in our minds, day by day and night by night. In our bodies and souls. We can still feel your presence. Watching our every move, listening to our every word. Do you hear and see us? Can you feel us?

We are all still missing you, and we will get through, even living without you, you are our strength and our pride, and only God may know why? But we will get by.

from *Eddie Hadden,* a poem, which he read at Service on November 24:

Who Will Carry the Flame
When it seemed our dreams would never take flight
You were the wind which gave us wings

When growing pains tested our fabric
You mended our fractures with your calm
When we felt homeless and dispossessed
You reminded us that our home is in each other
When we were without answers
You shared your great gift of enlightenment
When we were uncertain
Your words soothed us like a mother's caress
Now, that we must face a new future
We search our souls and ponder
Without the Firestarter,
Who will carry the flame
Your smiling face comes forth from our memory
ever the drum major, the sage, the cheerleader
Guiding us again to the light of awareness
"We shall carry the flame"
And the dream of the beloved community
Shall endure.
Goodbye, Lee

from *Jill Brody*, of Providence, RI, a friend from Star Island:

Evening services are always led by conferees. On the last evening of the Life on a Star I conference this past August, the husband of a couple that was conducting the service spoke about time, and his relationship to it, when he was told that he had a form of cancer which gave him a 2% chance of survival. This man is a fine writer, a compelling speaker, a wonderful person, and he has survived.

Sitting in the front of the chapel was a group of us who had taken a singing workshop, and who had been asked to sing as part of the service. Lee and I were among those singing. I was sitting to the side of the chapel, on pews normally reserved for a choir, but since there were so many of us, we spilled into the front rows as well. Lee sat in the first row. My 19-year-old daughter sat on the floor in front of me, facing the congregation. She was transfixed by Lee, who sat with tears flowing the whole time, watching our friend deliver his extraordinary address to us.

Outside in the warm darkness, after the service, my daughter talked to me about being in that place and looking out at all those people who had known her since she was a baby. She spoke about the night before, when she had come into the snack bar sometime after midnight to find Lee, Wally, and me, in our usual late night conversation. She commented on how much fun it was to talk to Lee, and about how she had not felt the least self-conscious in bringing out her brand new ballet point slippers, and dancing for us, wobbly as she was. "I was thinking about that as I was watching her tonight," she said, "and how she looked so beautiful sitting there crying. I never thought of tears being a sign of strength before."

from *Jerry Meyer*:

REQUIEM FOR LEE

Rest now, Lady Minister.
    Snuffed out with shocking suddenness
    that leaves us unbelieving and bereft.
But rest now.
    No good work is ever lost
    but lives in those that it has touched
    and is, unknowing, passed on by them
    so that it never dies.
So live.
    Live in the light that somehow came to you
    and that you shared so beautifully.
    We have no choice but to pass it on
    since it is now part of us.
So rest and live, Lady Minister.

from *Meg and Dick LeSchack*, of Lexington, MA, friends from Star Island:

Lee was for many years a prime mover in the hilarious end-of-week skits that highlighted the features and foibles of that year's chair people, theme speaker, and special events. I don't remember the theme, but one memory I have is of Lee bedecked in white tresses thanks to the fulsome strings of a janitor's mop. And the costume may have included some wittily arranged draping of sequins and satin (wherever did she manage to find these things on Star?) to suggest a primly seductive mermaid. She was note-taker of the innocent and earnest speaker's mannerisms and favorite expressions, co-conspiratorial author, co-impresario, and often the spirited narrator of the final production.

When I remember her, she's all ablaze, and like one of those trick birthday candles that keeps reigniting, she just won't stay puffed out. I guess that's a testament to the light she was, the light she shared, and the light that anyone blessed to know here will carry from her. But boy, it hurts like hell...

from *Martha Paradis Evans*:

When I think about Lee, the two words that immediately come to mind are grace and grit. I know th : some parts of her life were terribly difficult, yet there she was with the kind of serenity I marveled at. When I talked to her of sorrow and loss, her words spoke always to the triumph of the human spirit over fear and despair.
I wish I had known her longer and I ache for her family. Yet I believe that anytime anyone of us who was touched by Lee acts with integrity, strength and compassion, we once again are with the essence of Lee.

from *May Stawsky:*
Dear Lee,

We lingered at the door, extending our "good-byes," even though those good-byes weren't endings, more like the middle or even the beginnings of certainly unfinished conversations. You stood with your arms folded across your chest, the air was nippy: smiles moved across your face and your eyes flitted with a spark of mischief. I remember thinking I really should close the door because you must be getting cold-but I was having such a good time I really didn't want to leave.

I had come by the house to bring your plane tickets for our trip to Atlanta. On the phone we had worked out a time convenient to both of us, still I promised not to stay too long. Standing for a long time, trying to honor my promise not overstay my visit, but finally giving in to the gentleness of the moment I unzipped my jacket and sat down across from you in the rocking chair. We talked of many things, some serious, some light. Our words rambled easily, our ideas met and embraced, and we laughed; and we watched Friendly nibble at the tips of the aloe vera plant. Such a simple meeting, made extraordinary and joyous for me because of your wisdom and love.

The gradual waning light of the autumn afternoon, the deep red and white of the flowering plants against the dark wood, Friendly weaving in and about, and you, Lee filling the room with your peace, and strength, and love, and joy in all of us.

Wally came in from raking leaves and I knew it was really time to go. Conversation continued, now with the three of us, even after I had stood up and began to inch my way toward the door...and then those last few moments-just you Lee and I, finding it so hard to break away. We were still tossing words to each other as I went down the stairs to my car, smiling.

Love, May

from *Louise Lasota:*

Lee hated when people fussed over her about her health and this year seemed to be a particularly difficult challenge, health-wise. She always wanted to be viewed as the pillar of strength that we could all turn to and when she couldn't, it was frustrating to her. Now she's invincible. She has disbursed her energy and her love to each one of us and there is now an unlimited supply of both. She's passed the torch on to us forcing us to grow up and to stop hanging on to her skirts. We must take on the journey to make our vision one we can share with everyone. We don't make this journey alone though. Everything I do, I'll be checking in with her.

from *Dave Pleuler, Eileen Murphy, Devin, Rosey and Claire*, of Gloucester, MA, former UUSPers:

The light that Lee has lit in all of us has become a burning flame as fiery as her red hair. This light is a beacon that will always burn brightly when we are together as well as when we are far apart.

from *Cori Hoffman*, of Fair Haven, NJ, friend from Star Island:

Lee was a colleague, but mostly she was a friend from Star Island, her "spirit's home" and mine. I will always remember her warmth, her humor and her gentle way with children. She often did the children's chapel on Star. But, mostly, I will remember Lee with feathered mask and red hair flowing down in the gazebo telling fortunes at the children's carnival.

She will be missed by so many people.

from *Colleen Novosielski*, of Rutherford, NJ, friend from Star Island:

My husband Gary and myself and our two children were fortunate to have spent a week with the Reid's out at Star Island for the past five summers.

Star was one of Lee's favorite places and I would always look for her radiant smile and trademark red hair blowing gently in the breeze as we disembarked from the ferry and walked down the pier. She had usually arrived the week before and always waited on the dock to greet the [conferees] with hugs and smiles.

One evening when an outdoor activity got canceled due to poor weather, we gathered inside for storytelling. Lee took the mike to tell us the story of "The Last Wedding on Star Island." Lee had us in stitches as she gave a deadpan account of this infamous misadventure and I do believe that she could have had a successful career as a standup comic if she *hadn't* entered the ministry.

NOTES ON THE SERMONS

A Sunday morning service at our congregation includes many facets, such as opening words, hymns, readings, congregants' joys and concerns and, of course the sermon. Rev. Lee Reid could really move the congregants with her sermons. She even won the best preacher award in her class at New York Theological Seminary, a school where the majority of the students are African American and Hispanic, and students are from many other denominational affiliations and theological viewpoints.

In our congregation, after the sermon, much time was given for comments and inferences which people had in reference to the sermon. Our members, and Rev. Reid, felt that this part was very important. Unfortunately, these were not recorded and thus were not included in this book. Also not included in this book are many readings and poems relating to the sermons. However, the sermons as printed here stand alone and are quite readable.

These sermons were typed from Rev. Reid's handwritten works or from tape recordings. (Lee didn't like using machines: typewriters, computers, cars, stereos with multiple buttons, etc.) Hopefully, my daughter Martha and I were able to capture the true words, spelled correctly, and the essence of Lee's sermons.

ALL SAINTS AND ALL SOULS

Today is Halloween, and I would guess that most of us think of this day as a time for children (and adults too!) to dress up in costumes and masks and go out house to house, trick or treating. For older kids, it's often a time for pranks, or perhaps some behavior considered inappropriate the rest of the year but somehow gotten away with on Halloween. When I was a kid soaping windows and water bag bombs were the thing. When my children were growing up it was shaving cream and eggs. I don't know what the latest is around here, though I've seen some beautiful festoons of toilet paper. I'm ready with bowls of candy for any children or teenagers that come to my door for treats, I hope, no tricks. The little ones will come at dusk, the older ones when it's good and dark. By ten p.m. it'll probably all be over until another year.

And tomorrow will just be Monday. Plain, old Monday. That's all. But, in my Roman Catholic childhood, it was the day after Halloween that was considered the important day. It was a holy day, All Saint's Day. And because it was an official holy day, we were required to attend mass. Groan, groan, that meant getting up really early after staying out late on Halloween. Not easy to do. I did not like All Saint's Day. In truth, all it ever meant and all I remember was the getting up early to go to mass before school What else it was about I didn't know and I really didn't care. And frankly, on those terms I still don't know. As a Unitarian Universalist I don't have to observe official holy days. I don't have to get up extra early on the morning after Halloween, and that's the way I like it.

So, why did I pick this topic, All Saints and All Souls, for my sermon this morning? Well, I got to thinking about how I didn't like All Saint's Day when I was a child, and that got me remembering that the day after All Saint's Day was another church special day, but we weren't required to attend mass. It was called All Soul's Day. And I remembered that I always wondered what was the difference between the two, other than one day you had to go to church, and one day you didn't. All Saint's, and All Soul's. Then as I was remembering won-

1

dering about that, I thought of how we came up for a name for this Society. And when we were going to start this brand new congregation, we needed a name so that we could have a phone number, and so that we could advertise. We didn't have a whole lot of people to think of a name and vote upon a name. So, a couple of us who are here present sat down to think of a name that could go into the phone book. Now I am going to use some bad words. It's Halloween and it's time to be naughty and be a little prankish, so I will tell you in truth what we thought as we brain-stormed to come up with names.

First we thought of the name Palisades because it was a nice sounding and a generally descriptive word. But it left enough room geographically since we hadn't found a place where we were going to meet. So we thought of Palisades Unitarian Universalist Church or Congregation, but that would be PUUC. And so most people speak in those terms, we would have had a Society named, PUKE. No! Then we thought of Palisades Unitarian Universalist Society, and that would be PUUS. No! So we put Palisades at the end, and that's how we became the Unitarian Universalist Society of the Palisades. But first, when we were brainstorming all sorts of other names, I remember that we came up with a pretty accurate name for a brand new, very, very tiny congregation: SOME SOULS. We thought that was pretty witty, SOME SOULS, but it would not be a good name for a Universalist congregation, which we are, as well as Unitarian. Because Universalism has always been based on the conviction that all souls, all people, are precious. Not some, but all. But that led me to today's topic, All Saints and All Souls.

There are several Unitarian Universalist societies named *All Souls*, but none named *All Saints*, that I know of. How exactly then, I wondered, is this term saint defined. Of course I went to my trusty dictionary and here's what I found. A saint is a person officially recognized by the Roman Catholic Church and certain other Christian churches as being entitled to public veneration and as being capable of interceding for humans on earth. The second definition is one who had been canonized. The third definition, any person who has died and gone to Heaven. The fourth, any baptized believer in Christ. And the fifth, a charitable, unselfish or patient person.

Now we probably all use that last definition. A saint with a small "s." Oh, what she went through, she has the patience of a saint: patient, long-suffering, charitable, unselfish. And some Christian churches also use saint with a small "s." In calling their members the saints, they are baptized believers. But I'm going to focus today on that more traditional definition, that first definition. A person officially recognized as a person entitled to public veneration, and capable of interceding, with God, for people who are not saints. That's what I grew up thinking that saints were, and I think that many people do think that way. The Catholic Church has a whole official process for creating saints. And when I was doing research on this sermon, I went to the library and read a book on creating saints. It was very interesting and I will not read it to you today. The process is called canonization. Any person up for sainthood must first of all, be dead. There lives must be investigated. Their conduct and their writings must be scrutinized. Witnesses would have to testify to their great and heroic virtue. And miracles wrought posthumously through their intercession, would have to be proved.

Within the church, there's a whole group of professionals whose job it is to investigate the lives and validate the required miracles of any prospective saint. And only after this lengthy investigation can a prospective saint be canonized, which means that the person is worthy of what is called "universal public cult." The Pope declares that the person is absolutely, for certain in Heaven, with God. And because of that certainty, people can pray to the saint for intercession by God on their behalf, and, they do. And they have their favorites. There are many, many saints to choose from. When a person has been officially declared a saint, they are given a Saint's Day, and all the days on the calendar are taken by at least one saint.

Now my mother, for example, has always prayed to Saint Jude. Saint Jude is the help of the hopeless. I was never sure what was so hopeless. Although, come to think of it, I remember my mother telling me that she prayed for me. I grew up in a Catholic family in a Catholic town, so I heard about many prayers to many saints for many kinds of intercessions or favors. For a date for the prom, for pimples to go away, for good grades, to make the team, or to make that free throw. Don't let the dog die. Don't let grandma, or father, or mother, die. Prayers for peace on earth. Intercession to make him stop hitting me. To make the pain go away. To make them love me. To help me make it one more day.

Really, I didn't know so much about the prayers of agony and shame and desperation. I heard mostly about popularity and winning, and wishes coming true. And it didn't make sense to me. I couldn't understand the idea of people nominated to be saints, floating around in Heaven, wherever it was, and begging some Santa type God to grant people's requests. We were also supposed to take inspiration from the lives of the saints, to emulate them, to learn from their example. And this, too, proved to be elusive to me. I didn't want to be like any of the saints I heard about, fasting, praying, wearing hair shirts, being poor and miserable, treated badly, and often killed in some horrible way, burned at the stake or worse. I had no interest in taking vows of chastity, poverty or obedience. Especially, I think, obedience. Or of living alone in the desert. No. Sainthood did not appeal to me. And I didn't think that this is where the lessons of life were to be learned.

Perhaps if the stories and the morals had been put just a bit differently, as they are by Charles Merrill Smith in his book, *When the Saints Go Marching Out*, that I read to you earlier. Perhaps if I had read some of those practical lessons from the saints, I might have felt differently. Smith tells about Saint George, for example. And we all know the story of Saint George and the Dragon. A dragon was terrorizing the town, and could be appeased only by being fed sheep and an occasional maiden. George volunteered to slay the dragon. So he made the sign of the cross and galloped forth, brandishing his sword. And as he approached the dragon, it opened it's mouth and it gave a mighty roar, spewing out flames and clouds of smoke. We all know that part of the story. And here's the part we don't know. The smoke was so dense that it got in the dragon's eyes and he couldn't see. So George whacked off his head. The lesson, Smith says, for dragons as well as for us, is that you get in less trouble if you keep your mouth shut. That is a lesson I might have profited by then, and now.

Then there was Saint Polycarp, who was condemned to be burned alive. But he didn't mind, he didn't take much notice, because he had received divine insurance, that the flames wouldn't harm him. And sure enough, they didn't. He was bound to that stake, the fire was lit, but it didn't burn him up. So the officials put out the fire and stabbed him to death. The lesson here, fire insurance is important but you need other kinds of coverage as well.

And then there's Blessed Pellegrino. He was converted by Saint Francis and he lived a life of piety and humility. He is still invoked to this day to cure toothache. The lesson here is you can win local renown for piety and humility, but for an undying place in history, a toothache cure is better.

I never heard such practical wisdom about the saints. And I've left all that far behind. And yet, whether we call them saints, or heroes, or role models, or inspirational figures, we all need examples of lives well lived. Of people whose lives truly reflected their ideals, their values and their commitments. I would imagine that we each have saints, or heroes, or whatever we call them, I know I do. And we don't need for them to be canonized, or given official approval. They don't have to a have performed miracles. We don't want to pray to them. We don't ascribe any supernatural powers to them. We know that they are, or were, human and imperfect.

But something about the way they lived their lives, their failures as well as their successes. Their questions as well as their answers. Their vulnerability as well as their strength. Something, somehow, call it the truth of their lives, has touched us, has shown us something about ourselves, about our common humanity, in a way that gives us hope and courage. They remind us of the potential and the possibility that lives within each of us, for becoming more loving, more giving, more caring, more understanding, more open to that potential and that possibility in ourselves, and in others.

Some of our saints, our heroes, may be well known. Some of mine are. You might want to make a list. I did. The first person on my list was Rosa Parks. The second person was Martin Luther King, Jr. I added Gandhi, and Olympia Brown, who was the first woman ordained as a minister in this country, and was a Universalist. I added Dorothea Dix, who singlehandedly changed the treatment of the mentally ill in this country. I added Mother Theresa, because all my saints don't need to be dead. I added Barbara Jordan for the same reason. I added Arthur Mitchell, who some of you may know started the Dance Theater of Harlem, and opened up a whole new world of the Arts to many, many children. And I added Eleanor Roosevelt, because she was probably the first woman who I heard about as a child. She and Marion Anderson was also on my list. They stood up for what they believed in, and didn't think that it was inappropriate to speak out.

And some of our saints and some of our heroes are people known to very few., maybe just to us. Our friends or our family, a teacher, maybe a neighbor. Someone who said or did the right things when we were children. Who inspired us in ways that they may never know. And on that list I put my friend Maryann Bruce who has died but who I will never forget, because she was probably the example of just an ordinary person in my life, who did the most good. I put my mother on that list. And I put an elderly woman who I knew in the sixties, whose name was Charlotte Claflin. And I like the opportunity to mention her name, who nobody else here knows, but she's a saint to me. And on that list also, I put many of my friends, and my colleagues. We all have our saints, our heroes, our steadying rocks. And soon, All Saint's Day, I plan to take some time. I'm not going to wake up earlier than I have to, to do it. I plan to take some time to think about those people whose lives and examples have meant so much to me.

And I'll honor my Unitarian faith, which says that growth and change are always possible, and that each of us can add our bit to increase goodness and justice in the world. My Unitarian faith which preaches the message of hope. I plan to honor All Soul's Day too, as just as important. Traditionally, in the Roman Catholic Church, All Soul's Day is the day when the faithful pray for all the souls in purgatory, which could be just about anybody who isn't a saint. Who isn't, or who wasn't, perfect. I'll honor All Soul's Day for a quite different reason.

I'll honor my Universalist faith, which affirms the worth of every human person, every soul. Which preaches the message of universal love, and affirms the spark of sainthood in every person, in every soul, and which preaches a message of love.

I will honor my Unitarian Universalist faith, on these days, and I hope on every day, in which many people are making an honest attempt to break free of the hierarchical thinking which had formed and constricted so much of our human history. A faith where our saints, our exemplars and pioneers arise from among us and are named in our hearts and our actions, not by official pronouncement.

A faith in which we are all partners in the journey. A company of good souls, valuing all souls, believing in life and love, believing in ourselves and each other, celebrating the mystery and the oneness of the web of all existence, of which we are a part. John Murray, who founded the first Universalist church in America, wrote:

> "Go out into the highways and byways. Give the people something of your new vision. You may possess a small light, but uncover it, let it shine. Use it in order to bring more enlightenment and understanding to the hearts and minds of men and women. Give them not hell, but hope and courage. Preach the kindness and the everlasting love of God."

THE UNITARIAN UNIVERSALIST MINISTER AND THE POPE: A CONVERSATION

I was a little nervous about announcing the title and topic of this sermon. As some of you know, I announced a similar title and topic last fall, before the Pope's expected visit. And what happened? The Pope and I got sick and neither of us showed up at our appointed places. The Pope never got to New Jersey (never got to the United States!) and I never made it to the pulpit that Sunday, having completely lost my voice.

Well, whether the cause was viral or divine, The Pope and I never got to do our thing. This year, though, we've had better luck. The Pope had his turn, now I have mine. *Yes!* And here comes the Pope now! (A large, full size picture of the Pope was brought to the pulpit.) He is appearing today courtesy of one of our members. If you want to improve your image, enlarge your status, just see Richard after the service!

Good morning, John Paul. We are happy to have you here with us this morning at the Unitarian Universalist Society of the Palisades. I don't know how much you know about Unitarian Universalism, but if you had paid attention to our service so far and listened to our readings and hymns, and if you read the newsletters and brochures and membership packet I sent you (You did read them, I hope.), if you listened and read you should at least have a glimmer of what we're about. And don't forget to sign our guest book.

I have quite a few glimmers of what *you're* about. How could I help it! Newspapers. Magazines. Radio. Television. Your visit got great coverage. Did you know that we have three Richards in our Society, almost as many Richards as you have Gregorys. What? You have 13! Oh, I forgot. And you say you have 12 Piuses! But do you have any Linda's? We have 3! Oops..no, you wouldn't, not in your line of work. We'll get back to that later!

I'm glad you've agreed to be very informal today. (That's how we Unitarian Universalists are *every* day.) It would seem a bit much for me to call you Your Holiness and you to call me Your Majesty. "John Paul" and "Lee" seem much more cozier. We're pretty much come as you are around here, too, you can wear whatever you like. As you know, we are a welcoming and inclusive congregation. So here you are wearing a dress and I am wearing pants and that's just fine. (We'll get back to *that* later.)

And of course there's another reason I have quite a few glimmers of what you're about. Here I have the advantage, John Paul. You've never been a Unitarian Universalist, but I was raised as a Roman Catholic. Of course you weren't the Pope then, but I did hear a lot about *THE POPE*, generally speaking. In fact, what I heard helped move me right out of the Catholic church and into Unitarian Universalism. I mean no offense. I can see where it's fine for *you*, but I'm a *woman*.

Now let me say right here that I don't intend to be a Catholic basher. I mean no disrespect. Our first Unitarian Universalist Principle calls us to affirm the worth and dignity of every person. And have no fear, in all Unitarian Universalist history we have never tortured or killed anyone who disagreed with us theologically. And, in fact, we have many points of agreement. In your sermons and homilies last week you spoke in support of the poor, the disenfranchised, the weak and the sick. You urged people to be compassionate; to help others. You exhorted this country not to neglect the needy. You spoke of love as the greatest force for good. You urged support of the United Nations, that it be a home and a place of peace for all nations.

And I say *yes* to all this. I would hope that Catholics, Unitarian Universalists, *all* others would say yes to this, to love, to compassion, to justice, to our responsibility to one another. I would hope we would all, all, say *yes*. But John Paul, as a Unitarian Universalist minister, I would have to say that though we both aspire to the ideas of love, peace, compassion, justice..our motivation, our theological framework theological bedrock, our process, our way of being together in the world, are very different. Very different.

Throughout your talk last week you consistently put forth the message that you were speaking for, and to, the one true church, that acceptance of the bloody sacrifice of Jesus on the cross was the only way to God and salvation, that your church and its teachings are the avenue through which salvation is possible, that, in your words: Jesus established the church to be a sign and instrument of union with God and all of *man*kind. "The Lord, 'You said,' wants *his* church to make a home in the midst of every people, grafting the gifts of salvation onto the history of culture and each nation."

This church is hierarchical and patriarchal and you are the supreme leader. You speak for this Lord and *his* church, interpreting and insisting on your version of doctrine, theology and church rules. These things, you have firmly stated, are not open to debate. The church is not a democracy. The church teaches; the people obey. But they don't John Paul, they don't. It has been very interesting to me to read the various polls and surveys of American Catholics that have been published recently in various newspapers and magazines.

In the Sunday, October 1, *New York Times*: A survey reported that 67% of all Catholics surveyed said that they had a favorable opinion of the Pope, but only *16%* of all Catholics said the Pope's position on a social or political issue would make a difference to them. All the rest, 51%, don't care. The Pope's position would not influence their opinions or behavior at all.

Some typical responses: Said Ernest Schultz, a 67 year old retired oil field worker in Kingsland, Texas: It wouldn't make a difference at all if it (the Pope's teaching) wasn't to my liking. Nancy Cronin, a 35-year-old psychologist from Roseland, N.J., said, "I'm an individualist. To me, he's a figurehead, and that doesn't mean I agree with everything he espouses."

Catholics for Free Choice staged a protest march during your visit, John Paul, and they were joined by other groups - the National Abortion and Reproduction Rights Action League, ACT-UP, the Lesbian and Gay Papal Vigil Coalition, the National Organization for Women - all with many Catholic members. "The message the Pope is getting out is urging United States Catholics not to obey the laws in women's right to choose," one Catholic woman protester said. "What about contraception?" another asked, "Planet Earth cannot support an unlimited amount of people."

John Paul, these are questions: reproductive choice, contraception,

full and equal status of women, and of lesbians and gay men, ordina-
tion to the priesthood of any human beings who have discerned a call
or vocation rather than only unmarried, straight men. These are questions on which you have decreed there is to be no debate. Yet to me, a
Unitarian Universalist minister, these are *all* issues which have to do
with affirming the worth and dignity of every person.

This negative attitude about human sexuality is offensive to me.
It is wrong. And I certainly can't accept the idea of any God or any
religion purporting to speak for God which accords special privileges
to certain men and relegates every one else to second class or less.
Which condemns abortion and at the same time refuses to condone
responsible contraception, and so would consign millions of women
and children to lives of poverty and misery and the world to over-
crowding and depletion.

Which sets up a hierarchical institution as the only pathway to
God or spiritual fulfillment. Which tells people that they were born
in sin and only the church can provide the sacraments of salvation.
Which says nice words about caring for all the world's people and
then equates caring with proselytizing and conversion. Which speaks
of a loving God and then says, "My way or the highway!"

John Paul, you've had your say, too. You don't understand how we
Unitarian Universalists can consider ourselves religious or a religion
when we have no creedal tests for membership, no required beliefs,
not even in *God*, let alone Jesus Christ, the Trinity, saints, angels,
sacraments, heaven or hell. How we can believe that revelation is not
sealed, new truth is always coming into the world, into our consciousness. How we believe that mind, body and spirit are one, integrated, not polarized. How we believe we can and should question,
explore, think for ourselves, speak the truth in love and form a strong
spiritual community that celebrates our theological diversity.

I know that you can't understand or perhaps you just can't accept
that we are a profoundly religious and spiritual people. Trust me. It's
true. I don't mean to be judgmental here, or rude, but this is what fas-
cinates me: You seem to define/equate religion with rules. And your
people don't live by them. We Unitarian Universalists define our religion by our Unitarian Universalist principles. And we *do* live by them.
So, isn't it strange we, in our freedom, live by our principles. Your

people, in your structure of creed and doctrine and dogma, don't live by those rules. Freedom of belief, it's wonderful.

Today Unitarian Universalists across the continent are celebrating Ministry Sunday. Growing up a Catholic girl, I never thought I'd be a minister. Now I'm ordained and called to serve in the free church. This is a shared ministry, a circle, not a pyramid. We are all together in ministry.

John Paul, I know the pyramid's the only way for you. You have climbed to the peak. Your way is one way. Our's is another. I prefer the circle of life. I guess we each are where we want to be. Thank you for joining us this morning. I wish you peace and joy, and enlightenment.

REVELATION IS NOT SEALED

I'LL BEGIN WITH SOME typical comments I've heard about the Bible:

The Bible:
    Reminds me of my childhood.
    Comforting
    Inspiring
    Promotes guilt, sexism, racism and homophobia
    Essential literary resource
    Nonsense
    Never thought about it
    I keep meaning to read it
    My grandmother had one
    The basis of Western culture
    It sounds nice, but what does it mean?

The Bible: What *does* it mean? What can it *mean*? Let's explore.

A generation ago, at a Unitarian or a Universalist church service it would have been assumed that most of the people present, and most religious liberals in general, had a basic acquaintance with the Bible. It would have been assumed that most of the people present were from a Protestant tradition, had attended Sunday School as children and had been told the basic Bible stories that were, and still are, in many cases, part of Protestant religious education. How many of you heard those Bible stories as children?

Those of you who heard these stories know just what I'm referring to. But frankly, I don't know what I am referring to. By saying "Bible Stories" I can evoke a fairly common memory in the people who went to Sunday School. For me, however, as for others I'm sure, the only thing I remember when I hear about Bible Stories is those pamphlets, or whatever they were called, with colorful pictures, those Biblical illustrations, on the front page. My friends got them every week at Methodist and Lutheran Sunday School. The pictures were reproductions of religious paintings, some art, some not, I think. The Last Supper, Jesus in the Garden, Jesus with the Little Children, Baby Moses in a basket in the bulrushes, I still remember those pictures. I think I remember them so well because I didn't get any. And I remember those particular pictures because I knew what the topics were. But there were lots of others, of old bearded men in colorful robes and such- that had no meaning to me. I had no idea what they were about, because I didn't go to a Sunday School that taught the Bible.

I went to Catholic Religious Instruction classes where I learned the Catechism and the rules of the Church. And a real lack, I thought, there were no colorful pictures. No stories, either, that I can remember. At that time, in that diocese, we were told *not* to read the Bible. The nuns used to tell us not to read those Bible story pamphlets from the Protestant Sunday Schools. Why? Because, we were told, our church had the one true version of the Bible and it was not contaminated by individual interpretation. We heard the gospels read at Sunday Mass, with a homily by the priest. That was all we needed to know. We were supposed to have a missal with Latin text in one column and English in the other, so that we could follow the Mass, which was then in Latin, and keep our minds correctly focused.

So I grew up a Biblical illiterate. I never heard Bible quotations. I never heard the Bible used as justification for human behavior, that was the job of the catechism. I was a voracious reader, but I never realized how much of the literature and poetry I read was Biblically based. And when I rejected the religion of my childhood, rejected what I had come to feel was exclusionary, patriarchal and sexist, the Bible was right up there with the Catechism as something I did not need and did not want.

When I found Unitarian Universalism, I found my true religious home. In my UU community I was not an outsider who read too much, thought too much, questioned too much. There were many people there who were very much like me. We had rejected much of our religious past and were overjoyed to find that here we could be honest, open, free, or free-er, of hypocrisy; of paying lip service to an outworn past. We celebrated that freedom and we sought to build our own personal theologies or value systems within that accepting, non judgmental community.

Nobody ever said anything about the Bible, except once in awhile maybe someone would mention it was a *literary* resource. But spiritual resource? At least in the Unitarian Universalist circles in which I moved, no. And I was perfectly happy with that for 20 years until I went to seminary to study for my Master of Divinity degree in preparation for being ordained as a UU. And there, for the first time, really, I encountered the Bible. And it was a fascinating, enriching experience. My seminary, New York Theological Seminary, is non-denominational. It is urban, about 70% black and Hispanic when I attended. The theological focus was one of Biblically based social justice. And believe me, it's quite an experience to encounter the Bible for the first time on those terms.

A significant number of my classmates were from evangelical or Pentecostal or Fundamentalist or various orthodox religious traditions. Others were from mainstream Protestant churches. A few were Roman Catholic. Two of us were Unitarian Universalist. Only one person was Biblically illiterate. *Me.* Yet all of us were confronted and challenged by this Bible in which the Hebrew Prophets and Jesus were champions of the poor and oppressed and the outsider. A Bible which said that love and justice must be extended to all people and that racism, sexism, class-ism and homophobia were *wrong*. A Bible that said: Don't be smug. Nobody's perfect. Everybody's got some growing and changing to do. This means *you*. Who do *you* oppress? Who do *you* exclude? Who, and how, do *you* love?

And as we struggled together to understand the challenge in the light of our commitment to *ministry*, we shared something very powerful that certainly, for me, anyhow, was a transforming experience that has shaped my vision of ministry and of Unitarian Universalism. I learned that the Bible isn't a *bad* book. It isn't a *good* book. It's a book about the human struggle to find meaning; to struggle with those big questions:

How did it all begin?
How will it all end?
Why am I here?
Why must I die
How shall I live ?

Why is there evil? Violence? Suffering?
How do I know what is right?

And as we studied the Bible together we found that all of us, no matter what our religious tradition, our theology, our denomination, all of us, from fundamentalist to radical, were dealing with those very same questions in our own lives, today. And the Bible gave us a way to talk together; to share our stories and our struggles, our faith and our doubts.

In the process, I have *not* been converted to a Biblically based religion. I do *not* believe that the Bible is the final authority for theology, for preaching, or for living our lives.

What I have realized is that the Bible is more than a literary resource. More than a collection of stories. The Bible has been a very powerful influence in our culture, and has been both a negative force and a positive force. It has been used by individuals and by the religious and political establishment to manipulate and control, to justify the worst excesses and the most subtle cruelties. It has also comforted people and called forth the best within them.

In any case, it has played a large part in shaping the Western culture in which we live. If we ignore the Bible, we cannot understand this culture as fully as we need to, and we cannot fully appreciate the Judeo-Christian religious roots from which Unitarian Universalism has developed. When, for example, Unitarianism first came into existence during the Reformation, in was in protest about interpretation of the Holy Scriptures, arguing that the doctrine of the Trinity was nowhere explicitly taught in the Bible.

Michael Servetus, who wrote a book on the errors of the Trinity, was put to death for his beliefs as were others. Yet the reason for there protest was more than simple rebellion against ecclesiastical authority. These early Unitarians believed that a clearer, simpler, more accurate interpretation of the Bible would result in a more ethical Christianity.

Biblical interpretation was also at the heart of the development of nineteenth century Unitarianism and Universalism in America, as these liberal Christians characterized their religion as being the religion *of* Jesus rather than *about* Jesus, seeing Jesus as a great teacher and role model to be emulated rather than a divinity to be worshiped.

From this point, the Unitarian and Universalist religious perspective widened to embrace the concept that revelation is not sealed. That is, that new truth is constantly being revealed, that religious truth is not confined to Christianity and that there are many paths to God and to religious understanding and spiritual growth, many sources other than the Judeo-Christian Bible. We continue that tradition of freedom and discovery today. And this means that our worship, our preaching, our religious education, do not focus directly on the Bible. Our children don't receive those pamphlets with colorful Bible pictures and stories any more than I did way, way, way back then.

But there is a difference. I wasn't supposed to read the Bible because I couldn't be trusted to make a "correct" interpretation. Unitarian Universalist religious education is based on the child's experience of wonder and questioning. It stresses the building of self esteem, finding connectedness to others and to nature, and developing and understanding and appreciation of both the diversity and the unity of the world's people.

That's what we adults try to do, too. We place great value on religious freedom, on the freedom of each person to develop his or her own personal theology. No scripture, no book, no dogma, no doctrine has the final authority for us. That final authority lies in individual conscience.

We can't say to our children or ourselves it's true because the Bible says its true. But there's a lot we *can* say, and think about and explore. Sometimes Unitarian Universalists seem to have found it easier to teach our children about "other" in quotes cultures and religions. And that's important. It's one of the things that UUism does well and our children gain understanding and enrichment that is not easily found elsewhere. But in order to put it all together, to really make those connections, they (and we) need to feel at home in their own religious and cultural traditions as well, those of their family history, and those that the family has chosen for their own lives.

Unitarian Universalism has developed as a religion of reason, in reaction to idolatry and supernaturalism. If we were taught religion or the Bible in a way that stressed idolatry or supernaturalism, if our personal experience of the Bible has been negative; if we have seen it used to promote intolerance of bigotry or injustice; if indeed we have seen racism, sexism, homophobia justified by those who quote the Bible, chapter and verse, then surely the Bible doesn't have much appeal for us. And if, as in my case, we've simply never known or cared much one way or the other, there doesn't seem much reason to start now.

But I think it's worth taking a second look, or a first look, as the case may be. I say this for several reasons. First of all, the Bible as literature has much to recommend it As the basis for so much of our western literature and poetry, it is worth exploring. As you do so, you will be amazed at the huge number of quotations from great literature you'll find! At least that's how it feels to someone who comes to the Bible by way of the English Department and the Public Library.

You will also be amazed at the amount of religious symbolism contained in so much of what you have read. Northrop Frye, in his fascinating book *The Great Code: the Bible and Literature* points out, for example, that William Blake's line "O Earth, O Earth return" contains only five words and only three different words, yet contains at least seven direct allusions to the Bible. Don't ask me what they are, I'm only a beginner. But even on the rank amateur level, I've been rather non-plussed, to tell the truth, to find that I'd read so much without ever realizing where it came from, and so, many times, missing the deeper meaning or the subtleties of the passage.

Well all this is very Unitarian, don't you think? Read the Bible it'll make you more knowledgeable, improve your literary insights. But there's more. Much more. For me, the Bible is a human document, that is, written by humans, in whatever thought patterns and from whatever cultural perspectives were characteristic at the time that particular person wrote. Often the writer was recording a story or events that had been handed down in an oral tradition for many years, often many generations. And each generation added its own shadings and manner so that by the time it was written down it was already the product of many different minds, experiences and eras. This is most true of the Hebrew Bible or Old Testament The New Testament was written over a shorter period of time but was still, for the most part, a report of earlier events.

And so when we read the Bible we are not reading *a* book but many. Not *an* author but many. We are reading long stretches of history, and the voices of many. The Bible is a record of the human struggle to make sense of the world, of the human condition. We can never know what it is like to live in a different time, to live when our technology and culture didn't exist; before history was recorded. Yet the Bible has its roots that far back, and we can at least catch glimpses of that earlier humanity. I value that connection. I don't venerate it as the infallible word of a transcendent God, but to the extent that I define God as present in each yet greater than all, I can see the Bible as a way to make contact, however tenuous and partial, with that power, that creative spirit of life.

Each generation has aspired to make that contact. That's why we have religion. Every generation has had so many questions; so many fears and dreams and hopes and disappointments. That's why we have religion. That's why we have many religions, many interpretations of religion.

According to my definition, the only way we have of experiencing God is in relationship to each other in an honest, open trusting encounter. That's not easy to do at work or a meeting or during most of our busy days, even when we try. It's not easy to do even here in this congregation. But we are able to do it often enough to know its possible and it's necessary and it's worth the effort.

The purpose of our religion, I think, and certainly of this congregation, is to help us find ways to make that contact, to connect to relate to each other in ways that really will help us find God in our midst. One way we can do that is to give ourselves a time and place to be together and a focus that helps us to get beyond our surface contacts, our trivial yet necessary concerns of daily life, and go deeper into our minds and hearts to our spiritual selves, and then to share what we find.

That's why I'm a minister, to help us do that. That's why we come here, we want to do that. And that's why I want to facilitate our Adult Education programs. I hope that as we meet in our Unitarian Universalist Genesis Bible Study group and our Kindred Spirits group and other groups, we will find ways, as people have throughout history, to share our spirits, to meet in ways that will nurture and sustain us. It doesn't need to be earth shaking, this encounter with each other and with the spirit within and among us. It may be quite simple. But it will be good.

As Unitarian Universalists, or as people who care, we have the freedom to claim the Bible, as well as whatever else we need for ourselves. It does not belong to any one sect or creed. It is not what anyone else says it is. It is ours to interpret and it is ours to accept or reject or question or appreciate as we will.

> Revelation is not sealed
> And it will always be so!

LISTENING

It seems we all have two voices, the one we use in talking to others, and the one inside our head that is almost always talking to our self! Yes, we *do* hear that still, small voice that is our soul, our spirit, our essence, our conscience, our consciousness. We *do* hear that voice still and small that is deep inside all, each soul, each spirit, each essence, each conscience, each consciousness. But we must learn to listen. For that still, small, voice can be drowned out by the chatter and the clatter, the hurry and the worry, the clocks and the calendars of our daily lives. And we must listen to others, too!

Our schedules don't leave much time for listening. I'm reminded of my friend Peggy. She was a very busy and conscientious person wife, mother of six, community volunteer; she was so busy she hardly sat down, except when she was driving her kids to all their various activities. Even then it was hardly like sitting down; she drove a van and it was always full of kids, usually all talking at once loudly.

Well, anyhow, Peggy, who thought she was invincible, got a cold. And she couldn't stop to take care of herself, of course; she was much too busy; taking care of every body and every thing except herself. So she sneezed and coughed and just kept on coughing and finally surprise! She developed pneumonia. Then she *had* to stop. Had to stay still. Had to pay attention to herself.

Her family had to get themselves up, get their own breakfast, get out and on their way to school and work. And they did! With a lot of noise and confusion and every body bossing every body else around... And then, they were all gone, and it was quiet! Really quiet! Peggy laid there in her bed. She felt weak and sick; but she felt *peaceful*. At first she didn't know that's how she was feeling, because she hadn't felt that way in so long. She thought maybe she was delirious . She could hear birds chirping. She could hear the wind in the trees. And that was about it. She lay there, waiting, no! She wasn't delirious. She felt warm, though. Was her fever rising? No! The sun was shining in the window right on Peggy in her bed. Then she heard a voice, well, a sigh. AAHHH.

Then a whisper, was it a whisper? It seemed to be coming from deep inside Peggy! No, that wasn't it. She relaxed and listened, and this tiny, soft whisper came to her again. She tried to hear what it was saying but it wasn't really words. It was a whisper, like singing, like smiling, like praying. It was peace and it was love.

We all need to take time to listen to the still, small voice listen to the spirit of life and love that lives within each one of us and that exists among us, between us, within and without.

We are, most of us, people of words. Many words. We talk them and more and more we fax and e-mail them. All those words, but how many of those words are words of love? How many are words of sharing our true selves, how many of all those words are spoken face to face, heart to heart; how many of those words tell our stories, our hopes and dreams, our fears? How many of those words affirm, comfort, forgive, heal...

And how many of those words judge, push, coerce, direct, how many of those words say hurry up, just state the facts, shut up, go away, not now, keep out? How many of those words say *yes*. How many of those words say *no*? We are people of *words*. And when we are brave enough to speak our truth, to struggle to connect, who will be listening?

When my friend Peggy lay there that morning in her bed, sick, weak, but filled with and incredibly sweet and moving sense of love and joy, the phone rang. She answered it. It was a friend from the Library Board. Peggy! How *are* you?

Well, Joan, actually I'm in bed with pneumonia.

Good! Good! Now here's what I need you to do... THUD. Fortunately Peggy has a great sense of humor. Even so, this story is all too likely to happen *to* us or by *us*.

The quotation in our order of service today says: If it is language that makes us human, one half of language is to listen. And in order to really listen, we must pay attention. Listening doesn't mean just sitting there like a silent stone. We all know what it feels like to talk to that stone. Stone face, stone ears, No.

Listening is an active process. Listening means *giving. Responding.* It doesn't mean giving *advice* unless it's requested. It doesn't mean fixing whatever or whoever is wrong, in our eyes. It doesn't mean judging.

Listening means that we try to understand what the other person is telling us, without making it seem like a cross-examination. Listening means never negating or discounting another's feelings. Never telling them how *not* to feel.

Listening means, also, that we keep confidences. That we don't become a conduit for broadcasting some one else's thoughts, troubles or stories. Listening means respect. And sometimes listening can mean sharing silence together. In times of illness, loss, grief, sometimes there are just no words to say. Just a hand to hold. Just the warmth and caring presence of a friend.

As Unitarian Universalists trying to build a diverse and inclusive society, we recognize and affirm that each of us, each person, has a song to sing; a story to tell, a particular tradition and history and cultural viewpoint to share. We know that this is true of every person in the world, and we know that if we want to live peacefully and productively in that world, if we want to live out our principles of respect for every person, with liberty and justice for all, then we have to do everything we can to listen to each other's stories, learn about each other's culture and traditions, share our hopes and fears and dreams.

And it starts here. The world is a big place. But if we can come together in this small society and truly welcome and affirm diversity, truly listen to and learn from one another, if we can do that then we know that others can also. We know that our Unitarian Universalist principles are not just nice words on the back of our order of service but are ideals that can be lived out and lived up to. That can happen *only* in community. There is no way we can do this by ourselves.

And so as we share our music our songs today. We are also sharing our hopes and dreams that through our trying to know and understand and appreciate one another we are building a better world. We are affirming that every time we reach out to one another in openness and trust, yes, we are making the world a better place. Believe it!

The quotation in our order of service today says, "If it is language that makes us human, one half of language is to listen." And in order to really listen, we must *pay attention*. Listening doesn't mean just sitting there like a silent stone. We all know what it feels like to talk to that stone. Stone face, stone ears. No. Listening is an active process. Listening means *giving. Responding*. It doesn't mean giving advice unless it's requested. It doesn't mean fixing whatever, or who ever, is wrong, in our eyes. It doesn't mean judging.

Again, listening means that we try to understand what the other person is telling us, without making it seem like a cross examination. Listening means never negating or discounting another's feelings. Never telling them how *not* to feel. Listening means, also, that we keep confidences. That we don't become a conduit for broadcasting someone else's thoughts, troubles or stories. Listening means respect.

And sometimes listening can mean sharing silence together. In times of illness, loss, grief, sometimes there are just no words to say. Just a hand to hold. Just the warmth and caring of a friend.

WE STRETCH FORTH OUR HANDS

There were two stories in the *New York Times* on Friday. The first story was abut the efforts by leaders of a South Georgia Baptist church to disinter the body of a mixed-race (bi-racial) baby who was buried in the church's all-white cemetery and the second story was about a young man from Ashland, Wisconsin, who was harassed, tormented and beaten throughout his high school career, because he was gay. Despite his complaints to school authorities, and his parents' complaints as well, his tormentors were never disciplined. His journey through high school became a daily battle for survival and after two suicide attempts, he dropped out in 1993 and moved to Minneapolis on his own. He was only seventeen.

Never doubt that our commitment to diversity, to freedom, justice, compassion and respect for all, isn't important and necessary. Incidents like these reported in the *Times* are all too common. We know it is said that 11:00 A.M. on Sunday morning is the most segregated hour in America. And what is taught and modeled in the churches is lived out in the daily lives of many, to many, people. This is religion? For many, *yes*, this is religion. Well, I hope *you've* got religion. I hope *we've* got religion. A religion of love, compassion, understanding, and acceptance.

Now that you've found this religion, this congregation, the Unitarian Universalist Society of the Palisades, would you want to do without it? Would you want the people of Englewood and Teaneck and all the surrounding communities to lose the chance, the possibility, of finding a home here; finding a spiritual community that truly believes and practices Unity in Diversity; a congregation that lifts up and tries to live up to those Unitarian Universalist Principles? A congregation that endeavors to teach children these principles and helps them learn to live these values every day?

Aren't you proud, don't you feel a sense of hope and satisfaction that you are helping to support this congregation as we seek to live out our vision and reach out to share it with others? Picture what it would be like if this congregation; this loving, caring, sharing, daring community; ceased to exist. I would miss it terribly. Would you? I hope so.

I would miss it, YOU, terribly, and so I want to do all I can to make sure that the Unitarian Universalist Society of the Palisades thrives and grows. I hope you do too. I want to *support* this congregation with my time, my energy, and my money. I hope you do, too.

Unitarian Universalist minister John Wolf wrote:

A Reminder at Pledge Time

There is only *one* reason for joining a Unitarian Universalist Church! That is to *support* it. You want to support it because it stands against superstition and fear. Because it points to what is noblest and best in human life. Because it is open to men and women of whatever race, creed, color or place of origin.

You want to support a Unitarian Universalist Church because it has a free pulpit. Because you can hear ideas expressed there which would cost any other minister his or her job. You want to support it because it is a place where children can come without being saddled with guilt or terrified of some "celestial Peeping - Tom," where they can learn that religion is for joy, for comfort, for gratitude and love.

You want to support it because it is a place where walls between people are torn down rather than built-up. Because it is a place for the religious displaced persons of our times, the refugees from mixed marriages, the unwanted free thinkers and those who insist against orthodoxy that they must work out their own beliefs.

You want to support a Unitarian Universalist Church because it is more concerned with human beings than with dogmas. Because it searches for the holy, rather than dwells on the depraved. Because it calls no one a sinner, yet knows how deep is the struggle in each person's breast and how great is the hunger for what is good.

You want to support a Unitarian Universalist Church because it can laugh. Because it stands for something in a day when religion is still more concerned with drinking and smoking than with prejudice and war. You want to support it because it calls you to worship what is truly worthy of your sacrifice.

Yes, there is only *one* reason for joining a Unitarian Universalist Church. *To support it* Will You?

Yes, I will. Will You?

A few years ago, we had a family who attended our services regularly. Their children were actively involved in our Religious Education program. The woman attended our Adult Education seminars. They attended our pot luck suppers. They came to me for counseling and advice. They made good friends and socialized. But they would not make a financial pledge. Their response to the canvass was, "We think religion should be free." And even though they took advantage of all the services we offered, they simply refused to acknowledge that *somebody* had to pay!

Religion should be free! *Yes!* Our religion should insure that we are free to think, choose, question. Free to include the rich diversity of humanity. Free of prejudice, guilt, shame, bigotry and hatred. Free to share, to give, to love. But religion should not be a free ride! You can't really have a religion unless you give your commitment and support. You, each of you, are free to choose; to decide for yourself how important your religion; your spiritual community is; how much the Unitarian Universalist Society of the Palisades is worth to you; how much you can give up in order to give generously.

I assume in our Unitarian Universalist Society of the Palisades we have a pretty wide range of incomes. I've never discussed your incomes with you, though you know, or will soon know, mine. It's always been easy for me to be up front about income because I was a public school teacher and our salary schedule was part of the school's annual budget, was negotiated with the school board and was published. A copy was posted at my school. All you had to know was the number of years I'd taught and you could just look on the chart and see what I earned.

Now I'm a minister and my salary is listed in our budget, a copy of which is given to everyone and voted on by every member. So, since my income has always been a matter of public record, I've never developed a don't tell attitude. *But,* most people I know, other than my teaching and ministry colleagues, would never dream of mentioning their incomes, or mine. It's considered bad form. Tacky at best, ignorant at worst. Traditionally, one of the guidelines for getting along socially had been the admonition not to talk about three things, politics, religion and money. But those are three subjects we, here in our Unitarian Universalist society, must talk about. Politics? Well, we don't give partisan political plugs from the pulpit, but we do pay attention to how the political process promotes or impedes social justice. And Religion? We certainly talk about that. For most of us, our religion is the way we live our lives and so it will always be a part of our conversation. And the third subject we must talk about? We're back to money.

Now, we know why we have to talk about money in our Palisades Society. We have to pay the bills! We have to pay for the rent and the minister's salary and for the newsletter and for religious education and to help support our denomination and to fund social action projects...It's our society. We create it, we care about it, we need it, we pay for it. No problem. We can put a budget together and talk about it just fine! But then comes the next step. When each one of us has to decide what our fair share is in supporting our Society. When each of us has to decide how much money we are going to pledge to support Palisades for the coming year.

And to do that, we may need to talk it over with someone, or some ones, from the Society. We want to make an informed decision. We're all in this together and we need to be open and honest about what we can and can't do.

I was once a member of a Unitarian Universalist society that was so uptight about money that they wouldn't have an offering. Newcomers had no clue as to how the society was funded. Once a year there was a pledge drive and people were politely asked to give what they could. They received a pledge form and were asked to fill it out and send it to the treasurer. Most newcomers thought that some sort of diocese or synod, or *something* paid for most of the society's needs. They were often shocked to find out, if they ever did, that all Unitarian Universalist societies are autonomous, raise all their own funds, pay their own bills. That their Unitarian Universalist society had only the money that the members pledged or raised.

I also belonged to a Unitarian Universalist society where the treasurer stood up during *every* Sunday Service and harangued people about money. Told how much came in that week in pledges. Told all their expenses. Told people they had to give more. Predicted disaster any day. He was such a gung ho treasurer that he called us at 8:00 a.m. on Thanksgiving morning to ask us about our pledge. Amazingly, Wally and I are still Unitarian Universalists!

Both of these stories were about the same Unitarian Universalist society. Why the change in personality? By the time that the gung ho treasurer left office and was transferred all the way to France by his employer, the people of the congregation were so stressed, guilty and angry that they just didn't want to discuss it *anymore*. And they didn't, not for several years. Not until their assets, and their members, were nearly gone. Then they had to make a choice, pay up or die. So they forced themselves to take an offering at the services, and no one objected! It went pretty well! So then they had a noticeable pledge drive. And people participated! They gave! And finally they were ready for a face-to-face canvass. Canvassers called on people in their homes and really *talked and listened* about money and about lots more.

That society increased its pledges by 30% and raised enough to have a full-time minister. And most of the canvassers volunteered to canvass again the following year. They finally found a balance that worked for them. They finally learned that talking about money doesn't mean harassing. Doesn't mean assigning guilt or blame. Doesn't mean doom saying. And talking about money doesn't mean whispering so softly no one can hear. Doesn't mean shame. Doesn't mean embarrassment.

Talking about money, they discovered, meant talking! And listening. And sharing information. And sharing experiences. And being honest. And telling their stories. And laughing. And feeling *good*. Here at Palisades, we're all pretty new. We have no shared traditions or habits, good or bad, that go back more than a few years. That can be a real advantage. We can consciously work to create traditions we really want. One of the things that many of us treasure about our society is our sharing time during our services...knowing that we have the opportunity to say what we are thinking and feeling and to listen to others do the same.

We are a caring, supportive and nurturing congregation. I've never heard anyone put someone else down. I've never *ever* heard anyone be cruel or mean or take out their frustrations on another person or on the society as a whole. No one has abused our sharing time. I think, I hope, that we *all* feel that we are heard, affirmed and respected. We take our freedom, and our responsibility, very seriously. We also take it with wit and good humor. I think there aren't many topics we can't discuss, many ideas and feelings we can't share. There are some topics that can be tough to deal with. I hope that our society will always be a place where tough topics are shared, and where tenderness is shared as well.

This is what I hope for our canvass:

I hope that each person will have the necessary information and perspective to be able to make the best pledge decision possible. I hope that people with a lot of money will give a lot of money! I hope that people who have small incomes, who have little money, will never feel that they are small people, that they have little to contribute. I hope that no one will feel that they've given too much, or too little, but that they have done the right thing. I hope that you'll each feel that you can ask questions; talk things over, any time, with your minister, with your canvasser, with the canvass leadership, with your board of trustees. If there is something you need to know, if you need more information, more clarification, more inspiration, please ask.

This is your congregation. Your community. Your spiritual home. It's not your place of employment. It's not a competition. It's not a cocktail party; we are not here to judge and be judged. We are here to love and be loved. To share what we have, what we are, what we hope, what we dream, what we need.

We stretch forth our hands, to give and to receive.
We stretch forth our hands with grace and generosity.
We stretch forth our hands with Faith, Hope and Love.
We build for ourselves.
We build for our children.
We build for all those yet unknown who will enter our congregation.

SPIRITUAL CRISES

One day last month, I received a phone call from Cynthia Ward, a Unitarian Universalist minister and a colleague of mine in our New York Metro District Chapter of the UU Ministers Association.

"Lee, she said, "I'm calling to make sure you're all set for March 4."

"March 4?"

"Yes, you know, the panel."

"The panel?"

"The panel discussion for our March 4 ministers' meeting. The panel you're on. Next week."

"The panel I'm on?"

"Lee, the panel you're on. The panel on "Crises in Faith."

"Crises in Faith? Cynthia, one of us may have a crisis right now. This is the first I've heard of this panel."

After a shocked silence and a few horrified gasps, Cynthia cooled down and told me more about the subject of the panel discussion; the panel in which the program committee had meant to ask me to participate. They'd put my name on the program last October. They just never told me!

The idea, Cynthia said, was to have 3 of us Unitarian Universalist ministers speak to our 40 or so assembled colleagues about a crisis in faith in our lives as ministers. I told her that I didn't think I'd experienced a crisis in faith recently, but she convinced me that I probably had, or I soon, very soon, would.

So I agreed to be on the panel, and I began some serious thinking about the term crisis in faith. What does it mean? What does it encompass? How do we define, and experience, and respond to, crisis in faith? And what would I have to say at our UU ministers' association panel discussion? My first thought was that my faith, my religious and spiritual grounding, the rock on which my life, my self exists, that faith has been very strong, very solid for a long time.

Well, isn't that nice. Is this Miss Pollyanna speaking? No, no, it's not. For as I thought about faith, my faith, I realized that while my faith has proven, over the years, to be strong and steady, my response to that faith, my living out of that faith, has not been easy.

But, what is faith, anyhow? My trusty *Oxford Dictionary* describes faith as reliance on trust, belief in a religious doctrine, a system of religious belief, loyalty, sincerity

The Bible, Letter of Paul to the Hebrews, ch. v. 11:1, says that faith is the substance of things hoped for, the evidence of things not seen.

George Sand wrote that faith is an excitement and an enthusiasm, it is a condition of intellectual magnificence to which we must cling as to a treasure and not squander in the small coin of empty words or exact a priggish argument.

And H.L. Mencken said that faith may be defined briefly as an illogical belief in the occurrence of the improbable.

Paul wrote in his letter to the Romans, in the new testament: The faith that you have, have as your own conviction. And that, surely, is a definition that we can share. Faith is a matter of personal conviction. Each of us encounters and defines faith in our own way.

But however we define faith, we have questions, doubts. However we define our faith, it is never really defined until put to the test. Will our faith sustain us in a crisis? What does sustain us in a crisis? As we answer that question, we can begin to explore and understand the real faith; the real meaning, that exists in the very core of our individual selves.

I have a friend who has led a charmed life. She is happy and healthy. She has a healthy marriage and family. She has a satisfying career and plenty of money. She serves her community. She has wonderful friends. She really does have a charmed life, and it scares her. She wonders if she could handle pain or grief or disaster. She's never had the misfortune, or the opportunity, to find out.

Most of us, like it or not, have found out. We've faced hard times and survived. And we've learned and grown in the process. How do we do it? If we were to each tell of a personal crisis in faith, we would find out that no two stories are quite the same. But I would guess that they would have one element in common. That element is the threat of change that exists to some degree in any crisis. Crisis changes us. Every crisis changes us. And change can mean loss. It can also mean gain.

Elisabeth Kubler-Ross uses the metaphor of windstorms to describe the crises and the resulting transitions of life. She notes that if there were no windstorms the beautiful colors and shapes of the great canyons would not exist.

Over our lifetimes, our spiritual selves are created, colored, shaped, revealed in our experiences of crisis and transition. Often our crises are precipitated by the loss of someone or something precious to us. Often our crises result in the loss of some part of ourselves. The Chinese character for the word CRISIS includes the symbols both for danger and for opportunity. Both are inherent in any crisis we encounter.

What is the danger in loss? Our personal identity; our sense of self, is strongly invested in the people and things we hold as precious; our family, friends, work, our favorite activities, our home, our community, our physical appearance, our youthfulness, our status. When any one of these is lost, the security of our identity is threatened.

What is the opportunity in crisis? What can we gain? In our culture, growing up and growing older require a changing sense of personal identity. A crisis that threatens the old picture of the self is also an opportunity for a new self to emerge, a self that is more mature and evolved. How we respond to our crises, how we learn and heal from them, empowers our formation as spiritual people.

As I have told you before, I found, as I grew up, that I simply couldn't accept or identify with many of the tenets, the practices and the theology of the religion in which I was raised. I saw how much it meant to my family, particularly my mother. I saw her go to confession, receive communion, say the rosary and pray novenas to change the negative things in her life. Saint Jude, help of the hopeless, was a favorite Saint. His picture hung on our wall; prayers and novenas petitioned for his intercession in our lives. These things were expressions of my mother's faith and I respected that. But they were not for me.

For several years, I rejected the whole idea of having, or finding, a religion. Of having, or needing, Faith. It just didn't seem relevant. Then our second daughter was born and when she was only one year old we discovered that this beautiful, innocent, precious child was physically handicapped. We were told, after a series of grueling, painful, frightening tests, that she would never walk.

I was grief stricken. And I was angry. So angry. And I new that I was right not to believe anymore in that god of my childhood. The god that judged and granted favors and took them away. The god that cold be persuaded in matters of life and suffering and death. But that experience didn't stop the anger. No, it was the beginning of my spiritual journey, my journey to faith.

For me, for many of us, that journey began with doubt, with questioning what we had been told to believe; with the realization that we could trust our experience, our insight and our reason and that this could free our spirits rather than damn them; let them soar rather than cage them in a web of shoulds and should nots. My journey led me to Unitarian Universalism, where my mind and my spirit were nourished and where I began to explore and develop the faith that was truly mine.

It was just at this point that I was told that I had very serious cancer. A friend of mine had just died of the same form of the disease. It was a shocking, awful time. Yet through it all, my developing faith sustained me. As it turned out, I didn't have cancer. But the experience changed my life. The experience of my own mortality and the experience of my own spiritual resources opened life to me more fully, more completely, than I had known possible.

And what were those spiritual resources? What was sustaining my faith?

My belief that I didn't need to know the answers.

My belief that I didn't need the assurance of heaven, of an after life.

My belief in doing the best we can in the here and now.

My belief that though I can't choose or control everything that happens to me, I can choose the meaning I will give to what happens.

My belief in the power of love and community.

My belief that I can make a difference, add my life to so many others tipping the balance scale towards goodness and justice.

My belief that this is immortality enough: to leave behind what love and care I can. I believe all that today and I believe more. I've learned more. My faith grows.

I think I went through a time of arrogance in my faith development. I didn't mean to be arrogant, and that's not how I'd have described it then. But now I realize that for a while I really thought I could do it all myself. That I was in control. I really didn't think about faith. I saw life in terms of works. "By their fruits ye shall know them." "We are what we do."

But while that faith sustained me in crisis, my crises had fairly positive outcomes. My daughter walked. I did not die. And other similar stories. I've learned through experience, by just living long enough, that every thing changes. Good times come. Enjoy them. They go. Bad times come. We will suffer. It passes. Joys do not stay. They leave wonderful memories and increase our store of hope. Wounds do not disappear. They heal but leave scars. Some will always hurt, but we will survive them and laugh again.

But over the years, I've also learned that crises are not dealt out fairly. Some people get more than their share, and still more. (Some children don't walk. Some mothers do die.) Some lives are filled with fear, horror, beyond my ability to imagine or understand.

And I don't know, can't know, if my faith would sustain me in such crises. I don't want to know. What I do know is that what faith has come to mean to me is more than just faith in myself, in my ability to create meaning, to try, to do good, to make a difference, to learn, to grow. All those things are good and true and I believe in them and value them.

But now it's not enough. Now I know there's more.

I need faith and works, not faith in works.

I came from a tradition that taught me that faith meant petitioning God, or St. Jude or the Blessed Virgin Mary, to change things, to make them better, make me happy, make my life work. I came into Unitarian Universalism, a religion that affirmed my faith in myself, in my ability to change things, make them better, make me happy, make my life work.

The next step was to develop my faith in others, to realize and rejoice in the fact that I can't do it all alone, that I need community, that we need each other, that together we have the ability to change things, make them better, make ourselves and others happy, to make life work.

And now, where am I now in my faith journey? I've learned, am learning, to accept that just as I can't always do it alone, we can't always do it better either. Even together sometimes we can't make it better, can't do what we want to do.

Sometimes we can't ease someone's pain, can't save their life. Can't make things better. Can't make them happy. All we can do is be there. Maybe we won't say the right thing. Maybe we won't do the right thing. Maybe all we do is share the silence. Or tears. But nothing, nothing, is more important than being there. And this means not just being there for others but letting others be there for us.

Sometimes the greatest gift we can give and the greatest faith we can have is to let someone into our lives, into our *trust*. Let them be with us just as we are, in our pain or shame or despair, in whatever shape or form we are in, no matter how unacceptable we think we are.

My daughter is grown now. Her life has not been easy. She has taught me more than she'll ever know. Recently, as many of you know, she had spinal surgery. It has left her with maximum pain and minimum function. Yes, she is certainly in the midst of a great physical and spiritual crisis. And yes, our family is experiencing great spiritual crisis, each responding in his or her own way yet all together in our hope for improvement, our compassion, our love and our frustration.

And yes, this is true for me as well. As a mother, and as a minister, I am called, body and soul, to heal. To alleviate pain and suffering. To make things better. To help my child, my family, my people, find meaning and hope and peace. And I am also called to share the pain, the fear, the anguish, anger, the waiting. I am called to make my life a chalice that will receive and hold every drop of what it means to be human. All the joy, all the pain. This is what we are all, each in our own way, called to do.

A few years ago, Margie, a young woman in my congregation who was dying of cancer, spent one of her last weeks at Star Island when I was also there. She told me that she wasn't afraid to die, but she was afraid of more suffering than she could handle. She wanted to be strong and peaceful.

We looked our over the ocean at the gulls. I suggested that she hold on to the image of the gull. The seagull flies and soars, and then rests on the water. She nestles down into the wave, not on top if it. No matter how rough and choppy the water, the gull trusts that she will be born up; supported. She settles in; doesn't flap her wings or fight the waves. She rides safely and is at one with the sea. And when the time is right, she soars into the infinite sky. Several times during the week, Margie would catch my eye and say, "I'm being a sea gull." The sea gull image keeps returning to me. Learning to have faith and trust in the midst of rough seas is not easy. But that's what we need to do. Sometimes in our lives we soar, fly free, and sometimes we need to rest in the choppy waters. Rest and wait, just be there, until one day it's time again for us to fly.

Margie and I talked about what she thought happens when we die. She told me she thought that we are united with a cosmic force of life and love, in universal oneness, of which we all are a part and in which we can never be separated.

I believe that this unity, this oneness, this connectedness, is what we yearn for in our daily lives in the here and now. And I believe that as we reach out to each other in love and trust, as we share our joys, our sorrows, our pain, our grief, we are not only meeting/connecting with each other but with God, ultimate reality, the creative force, the Spirit of Life. The spirit, by whatever name, or no name, we may use, of challenge, inspiration, justice, the spirit of compassion, solace, healing and hope. We are giving and receiving love in its highest , widest, deepest sense. It is that love, both the giving and the receiving, and my belief in the possibility of this love at any moment in our lives, that now sustains me in my crises in faith.

May it be so for you.

SEPTEMBER DAYS

Remember back when you were a child and a year was a very, very long, long time?

When one birthday to the next really was a whole year instead of what seems lately to be about a week? When you waited and waited for Christmas to finally come, or the last day of school, or some other wonderful event?

When I was a child, growing up, my family always made a big event of sighting the first robin each spring. We'd listen and look and scan every tree, every lawn until, finally, one of us would see the robin and rush home to report the good news. It really did seem like an important milestone, something I looked forward to each year.

Now, though, its different. I don't even notice that the robins have left, let alone that they've returned. The seasons flash by; the years are flashing by. The weeks, the days, the hours I think sometimes they're reaching the speed of light.

And I don't like it. I don't like it at all. I want more time! I need more time. I want time to slow down to a more leisurely pace. I want to experience, NOW, the long, slow anticipations of my childhood.

I want more time, but it seems that I have less and less. Do you ever feel that way? Is time rushing by for you, too? Do you ever wonder how you'll fit everything into your life? Are you faced with the realization that you won't fit it all in, that you can't fit it all in?

The fall is here again, already, and you are still wondering where the summer went. So many people tell me things like this. So many people seem to be struggling with big plans, big commitments, big needs, and tiny weeks, tiny days, tiny minutes. "I don't have time," they say, "I need more time..."

September. Yes, yes, September is the time when we become more aware of the passage of time. This is the season of change. The days grow shorter. Every day we notice that it gets dark a little earlier. The nights are cooler, and the mornings, too. There are no frosts yet, but the flowers know that the time is short. Some are blazing that last great burst of color. Some are already fading; or grown so full or

38

leggy that they are leaning and drooping.

And here , in New Jersey, it's still green, but there are a few hints of red and gold; a few leaves on lawns and pavements; and people are talking about trips north to "see the leaves." There are apples, beautiful apples, the kind that snap when you bite into them. And there are school buses and new shoes and new schedules and new committees....

It is harvest time in the natural world, a time to store up, to begin to draw inward, to conserve, to reflect, to focus on hearth and home. At the same time, in our culture, the academic and commercial calendars mark a time of beginnings; re-commitment; increased demands and effort.

And so September, autumn, may be a bitter sweet time. The changing season calls us, calls us deeply and powerfully, calls us to reflect, to ponder not only the seasons of the year but the seasons of our lives; the seasons of the spirit. We are gripped by the awareness of the brevity, and preciousness of each day; of each moment. And our duties, responsibilities, ambitions and options also call to us, call us to action. This need to reflect and this need to act can tug us in different directions; make us feel fragmented. We long for inner peace and harmony but feel instead a certain discordance and tension, tension between our curiosity about the future and our fear of the unknown, between our need for security and our wish for change, between our need for pleasure in storing up riches, treasures, memories, and our growing realization that it is indeed true that you can't take it with you; not even the memories. Between our need to feel powerful, in control, invincible, and our knowledge, however we try to deny it, that the cycles of nature, of birth and death, move in us and control our lives in ways we cannot control.

Those inevitable cycles are part of our life's journey, our life's task. This task, this journey, is something we all have in common. Where we differ is in how we go about our task, how we perceive it and how we act on it.

Remember the story of the grasshopper and the ant? Of course you do, if you were raised in this country. That story told us that there are two ways to live, there's the way of the grasshopper and the way of the ant. The way of the grasshopper is to live in the here and now. What can we do to enjoy today? We can't know what tomorrow will bring; or even if there will be a tomorrow. So let's enjoy today. The grasshopper hung out all day, making grasshopper music and spitting tobacco juice and making big leaps into the air; not to get anywhere in particular but just for the fun of leaping. The word is *now*. That's the way of the grasshopper.

Not so for the ant. The way of the ant is quite different, the ant always knows where it's going; the ant is purposeful. The way of the ant is the way of industry; of planning and working for the future. Today is lived only as preparation for tomorrow. Postpone pleasure and leisure, work hard and store up everything that might be needed in the future. The word is *later*. That's the way of the ant.

The two ways have traditionally been presented as mutually exclusive. We were to choose which of the ways we would live, and there really wasn't supposed to be much of a choice. There was the *good* or smart way and the *bad* or foolish way and it was assumed that it was easy to tell the difference.

It was good, it was smart to choose the way of the ant and it was foolish, very foolish, to choose the way of the grasshopper. Well, it's not that simple any more. And I don't know about you, but I refuse to choose one way over the other. I choose both. I want a sense of purpose and direction in my life. I want to plan for the future. I don't ever want to be an indigent old lady, dependent on the kindness of strangers, or relatives, or friends! I want to work for a better world for myself and every body else.

But I also want to enjoy each day as it comes, and savor every precious moment of love and tenderness and friendship, savor the sights and sounds and textures and smells of life, celebrate and treasure the great miracle of interconnectedness that we call the web of existence.

I want it all. I do. I want the community and purpose of the ant and the leaping freedom of the grasshopper. I want the commitment and I want the joy. Don't you? And it may be possible to have all these —sometimes. As long as we're willing to pay the price. To live with purpose and commitment, we have to be willing to risk disappointment and failure. Things will not always turn out as we expect, even if we do our best. And we won't always do our best, even when we want to. We must learn to be responsible but not judgmental, to be tough but not mean. We must learn discipline. We must learn sacrifice. And we must learn forgiveness.

To live with freedom and joy, we have to risk pain and loss..the price of vulnerability. When we leap for the pleasure of leaping, we may get hurt or lost. When we take time to savor life's pleasures, we may miss the opportunity to gain some material treasures. We must learn to enjoy life but not be self-indulgent; to live in the moment but not for the moment.

And we must not forget that sometimes, for some people, the choice is not purpose or commitment or freedom or joy, but survival, and then we must give or receive help however we can.

September is a time of endings and beginnings. It is a time of harvest and setting forth. It is a time of evaluating and planning. It is a time for us to bring our hopes and fears, our past and future, together in positive affirmation of each day. As we make life's journey, the journey through the cycles of life, we all need help and encouragement. Whether we are struggling to make it through our first day of kindergarten or a mid-life crisis or the last days of life, we need to know we're not alone.

May we help each other to learn to be fully present to each day, centered yet flexible hopeful and loving, imperfect but trying, willing to take time when we need it and give time when it matters. And may we affirm, together , as we reach out in affection and support, in an ever widening circle of love.

GROWING SOULS

The voice of loneliness. The human cry for connectedness, for love, for acceptance, for meaning, for purpose. The human cry yearning for what I call God. And the question contained in that cry, that human yearning: Is it possible that God cries out to me? And if so, how do I hear? And how do I respond? And how do I find connectedness and love and acceptance and meaning and purpose? Or rather, how do I participate in connectedness and love and acceptance and meaning and purpose? Is it in our yearning and asking the question how? Or is it in recognizing that we must participate, that we enter into the process of spiritual growth, the process which I call growing our souls?

Soul. It's another one of those loaded words for many of us. Loaded with all sorts of baggage from our past— Sunday school, religious instruction, catechism class, whatever religious training we received, whatever religious training we never received. I for example received what was probably a typical Catholic teaching about the soul and I interpreted this teaching in what I suspect was a typical child's way. And so for a long time I pictured my soul as a white something, a shape or a mass or a blob. Anyhow, it was real even though you couldn't see it and it existed inside of me in the vicinity of my heart. And every time I sinned, every time I 'committed a sin' as the terminology was in those days, a black mark appeared on my soul. The only way the black mark could be erased was by going to confession, confessing the sin, and reciting the prayers of penance assigned by the priest who had heard my confession. If I didn't go to confession my sin and all those black marks would just keep eating away at my soul until it was like Swiss cheese or pumice, and I guess eventually my soul would have just been blacked out or erased or eaten up. It was all sort of horrible and creepy and mean, somehow. I never had a good feeling about my soul, it was just sort of a blank on which bad stuff could be recorded, a sort of a judgment indicator.

My soul was also what got to go to heaven when I died if there were no mortal sins marking it up (in which case, of course, it would go to hell). I never quite made the connection that the "sin indicator soul" in my chest was whatever it was of me that could go to heaven or to hell. It just didn't seem to make much sense to me, it didn't add up. I couldn't really work up to being very scared or very worried, which I knew I was supposed to be.

And when I grew up, since none of this stuff had any meaning for me, any idea of soul or of having a soul just became a rejected dogma of my Catholic background, completely irrelevant to my adult life and my adult thought. But, at the same time, I was learning a new definition of soul completely different, the African-American soul, soulful, soul music, soul brother and sister, not having a soul but being a soul. It had nothing to do with what I thought of as religion. It wasn't something that set you apart; it wasn't a record of your sins; it was something that connected people. It was a shared identity — soul. I accepted that usage of the word soul. It was real, it was descriptive, and it was human. And that's the only soul that made sense to me for many, many years. And that soul still does make sense to me, but now, there's more. I've got a soul again. And it's not a white blob with black spots, it's not Swiss cheese, it's not pumice, it's not a Dalmatian look-alike. I remember when I saw my first Dalmatian all I could think of was my soul with black spots.

It is instead an integral part of every human being, not just me, and no religion owns it or controls it or defines it. It is what makes us brothers and sisters whatever our color or race or creed or sex or age or sexual preference, and it's what makes each of us our own true self. As far as soul goes, I've come a long way in my thinking and in my feeling and in my understanding and I still have a long way to go. The rest of my life, I think. Growing a soul takes a lifetime — that's what it's all about. How have I arrived at this acceptance of the idea of the human soul after rejecting it so completely for so long? Experience. Experience in being a loving, suffering, finite, fallible, laughing, hurting human being. Experience that has taught me that all human beings are like me and yet each of them is also unique. And we all share that human cry, that human longing for something vital, ineffable, unknown, precious. We share deep hunger and we share deep need.

And I ask myself what is this hunger, what is this need? Well, first of all of course life on its most basic level is about survival. I know that. And until those most basic survival needs are met — food, clothing, shelter — humans don't think about much else. But for most of us those basic survival needs are met. Maybe not as luxuriously or as fully as we'd like, but they are met. When that happens we move to the next level of needs and this is what I want to look at today. I mentioned earlier our need for love and acceptance and purpose and meaning but there is another need that is strong, very, very strong. The need for power and control. Our ego manifests itself in the need for power and control, our soul manifests itself in giving and receiving unconditional love.

We've been taught that we are the products of evolution. In the past the assumption seemed to be that we are the end products of evolution, at least certainly that's what I grew up thinking. Now, however, we've begun to realize that we are part of the process of evolution and it's probably never ending. Until recently, evolution has been seen as linear — a straight line upward into the future beginning with single celled creatures and progressing to more and more complex organisms up to human beings which are the most complex and therefore the most evolved. Evolution has been described as survival of the fittest. The organism that is the best able to control both its environment and all the other organisms in its environment and so is most able to ensure its own survival and serve its own self-preservation, that organism is the most evolved, that organism is the human being, us.

And we've long known that this definition of evolution is inadequate, but it's hard to know why. When two humans interact with one another, in terms of organizational complexity they are equally involved. They are equally evolved. If both have the same intelligence and yet one is small-minded and mean and selfish, while the other one is altruistic and magnanimous and kindly, we say that the one who is magnanimous and altruistic is the more evolved of the two. If one human being intentionally sacrifices his or her life to save another, for example, using his or her own body to shield another from an unseen bullet or speeding car, we say that the human who sacrificed his or her life indeed was one of the most evolved among us. We know these things to be true, but yet they are at variance with our understanding of evolution as survival of the fittest. Our deeper understanding tells us that a truly evolved being is one who values others more than it values itself and that values love more than it values the physical world and what is in it.

We must now bring our understanding of evolution into alignment with this deeper understanding by reflecting on a new and expanded understanding of evolution, one that validates those deepest truths that each of us hold. We can see what we can evolve into and what that means in terms of what we experience and how we value things and how we act. We can see the results, you might say, of our intentions. We see that rage kills; it takes away breath, the life force; it spills blood. We see that kindness nurtures. We see and feel the effects of a snarl and also of a smile. We experience our ability to process knowledge. We see, for example, that a stick is a tool and we see the effects of how we choose to use it. A club that kills can also drive a tent stake into the ground to hold a shelter. A spear that takes a life can be used as a lever to ease life's burdens. The knife that cuts into flesh can be used to cut cloth or carve wood. The hands that build bombs can be used to build schools.

The minds that coordinate the activities of violence can coordinate the activities of cooperation. We see that when the activities of life are infused with reverence, they come alive with meaning and with purpose. We see that when reverence is lacking from life's activities the result is cruelty, violence and loneliness. We come to understand what causes us to expand and what causes us to contract. What causes us to grow and what causes us to shrivel. What nourishes our souls and what depletes them. What works and what doesn't. But when the physical environment is seen only from the ego's point of view, physical survival appears to be the fundamental criterion of evolution because no other kind of evolution is known. And it's from this point of view that survival of the fittest appears to be synonymous with evolution and physical dominance appears to characterize evolution. Power to control the environment and those within the environment appears to be essential.

The need for physical dominance produces a type of competition that affects every aspect of our lives. It affects relationships between lovers, and between superpowers, between siblings and between races, between classes and between sexes. It disrupts the natural tendency towards harmony between nations and between friends. The same energy that sent warships to the Persian Gulf, sent soldiers to Vietnam and crusaders to Palestine, the energy that separated the family from Romeo from the family of Juliet, is the same energy that separates the racial family of the black husband from the racial family of the white wife. The energy that set Lee Harvey Oswald against John Kennedy is the same energy that set Cain against Abel. Brothers and sisters quarrel for the same reasons that corporations quarrel. They seek power over one another.

The power to control the environment and all within it is power over what can be felt, smelled, tasted, heard and seen. This type of power I would call external power. Now external power can be acquired, it can be lost as in the stock market or in an election. It can be bought or stolen, transferred, even inherited. It's thought of as something that can be gotten from some one or somewhere else. One person's gain of external power is perceived as another person's loss. The result of seeing power as external is violence and destruction. All of our institutions — social, economic and political — reflect that understanding of power as external. Families, like cultures, are patriarchal or matriarchal. One person wears the pants. Children learn this early and it shapes their lives.

Police departments, like the military, are produced by the perception of power as external. Badges, boots, rank, uniforms, weapons, radio are symbols of fear. Those who wear and use them are fearful. They fear to engage the world without defenses. Those who encounter these symbols are fearful, too. They fear the power of those symbols. Or they fear those whom they expect this power will control, or maybe they fear both.

The police and the military, like patriarchal and matriarchal families and cultures, are not origins of the perception of power as external, they are reflections of the way we have come to view power. Perception of power as external has shaped our economics. The ability to control economies within our communities and within nations, within our families, I think, and the ability to control the international economy within the world is concentrated in the hands of a very few people. To protect workers from those people we've created unions. To protect consumers we've created bureaucracies and governments. To protect the poor we've created welfare systems. This is a reflection of how we've come to perceive power. The possession of the few while the majority are its victims.

Money is also a symbol of this external power. Those who have the most money have the most ability to control their environment and those within it, while those who have the least money have the least ability to control their environment and those within it. Money is acquired, lost, stolen, inherited, and certainly fought for. Education and social status and fame and things that are owned, if we derive a sense of security from them are symbols of external power. Anything we fear to lose — a home, a car, an attractive body, an agile mind, a deep belief, is a symbol of external power.

What we fear is an increase of our vulnerability. And this results as seeing power as external. When power is seen as external, the hierarchies of our social and economic and political structures as well as the hierarchies of the universe are seen as indicators of who has power and who has no power. Those at the top appear to have the most power and therefore they are the most valuable and the least vulnerable. Those at the bottom seem to be the least powerful and therefore they are the least valuable and the most vulnerable. For in this perception the general is more valuable than the private. The executive is more valuable than the chauffeur. The doctor is more valuable than the receptionist. The parent is more valuable than the child. And the divine is more valuable than the worshiper.

We fear to transgress our parents or our bosses and our God. All perceptions of lesser and greater personal value result from this perception of power as external. Competition for external power lies at the heart of all violence. The secondary gain behind ideological conflicts such as capitalism versus communism and religious conflicts such as Irish Catholic versus Irish Protestant, Jew versus Arab, geographical conflicts, familial and marital conflicts, all are based on external power, its fears and its uses. The perception of power as external splinters our psyche, our souls. Whether it's the soul of the individual or the community or the nation or the world. There is no difference really between schizophrenia and a world at war. There is no difference between the agony of a splintered soul and the agony of a splintered family and the agony of a splintered nation.

When a husband and a wife, when lovers compete for power, they engage in the same dynamic that humans of one race do when they fear humans of another race. From these dynamics we've formed our present understanding of evolution as a process of ever-increasing ability to dominate the environment and to dominate each other. And after a millennia of brutality to one another individual to individual, group to group, it's now becoming clear to one another that the insecurity that underlies this perception of power can't be healed by more and more accumulation of that power. It is evident for all to see, not only with each newscast and every evening paper, but also through each of our countless suffering as individuals and as a species. The perception of power as external brings only pain and violence. And this is how we have evolved until now.

But our deeper understanding can now lead us to another kind of power. A power that loves life in every form that it appears. A power that does not judge what it encounters. A power that perceives meaningfulness and purpose in the smallest detail upon the earth. This is authentic power. When we align our thoughts and our emotions and our actions with the highest part of ourselves we are filled with enthusiasm, with purpose, and with meaning. Life is rich and full. We are joyously, intimately engaged with our world. This is the experience of authentic rather than external power. It has its roots in the deepest source of our being. An authentically empowered person will not make anyone a victim. An authentically empowered person is one who is strong. Strong enough not to need force as a way of relating to another person or to life.

Nineteenth Century Unitarianism and Universalism believed very, very strongly in the perfectibility of human nature and in the spark of the divine that existed in every human being. This contrasted strongly with the then prevalent Calvinist view of human nature as sinful and depraved, incapable of improvement let alone perfectibility, with the possibility of salvation only through the acceptance of Jesus Christ as the divine lord and savior. Unitarian Universalists have never accepted that negative view, but the terrible tragedies of holocausts, wars and weaponry, hunger, homelessness, drugs, AIDS, have challenged our theology of hope and progress. We've struggled to come to a new understanding of human life as an inextricable part of the interdependent web of all existence, constantly interacting, constantly changing and evolving and in which we can be a force, each of us, for beauty and truth and justice and goodness.

No understanding of evolution is adequate that doesn't have as its core that we are on a journey towards authentic power and that the authentic empowerment is the goal of our evolutionary progress and the purpose of our being. We are evolving from a species that pursues external power into, we hope, a species that pursues authentic power. It's in this new perspective that the origins of our deepest values are found. From this perspective the motivations of those who consciously sacrifice their lives for higher purposes makes sense. The power of Gandhi is explainable. The compassionate acts of Christ are comprehensible. All of our great teachers have spoken to us and acted in accordance with perceptions and values that reflect that larger perspective, and therefore their words and their actions awaken within us the recognition of authentic power.

From the old perception, we are alone in a universe that is physical. From the new perception, we are never alone and the universe is alive, conscious, intelligent and compassionate. From the old perception, the physical world is an unaccountable given in which we unaccountably find ourselves, and we strive to dominate it so that we can survive. From the new perception, the physical world is a learning environment that is created jointly by all the souls who share it and everything that occurs within it serves their learning.

From the old perception, intentions have no effects and the effects of actions are physical and not all actions effect us or others. From the new perception, the intention behind an action determines its effects. Every intention affects both us and others, and the effects extend far beyond our immediate world. The larger frame of reference allows an understanding of the meaningful distinction between the personality and the soul. Our personality is that part of us that we were born into and lives within us, and it will die, in time. To be a human and to have a personality are the same thing. Our personality, like our body, is the vehicle of our evolution. The decisions that we make and the actions that we take are the means by which we evolve.

At each moment, we chose the intentions that will shape our experiences and those things on which we will focus our attention. These choices affect our evolutionary process and this is true for each person. If we chose unconsciously, we evolve unconsciously. If we chose consciously, we evolve consciously. The fearful and violent emotions that have come to characterize human experience can be experienced only by the personality. Only the personality can feel anger, fear, hatred, vengeance, shame, regret, indifference, frustration, cynicism. Only the personality can judge and manipulate and exploit. Only the personality can pursue external power. The personality can also be loving and compassionate and wise in its relations with others. When a personality looks inside itself it finds a multitude of different currents or strands. Through experience, the personality learns to distinguish between these currents and to identify the emotional and psychological and physical effects that each might have. It learns, for example, which currents produce anger or destructive thoughts or actions and which currents produce love and healing thoughts and constructive actions. In time, it learns to value and identify with those currents that generate creativity and healing and love and to challenge and release those currents that create negativity and disharmony and violence.

In this way, a personality comes to experience the energy of its soul, to grow that soul. Our soul isn't a passive or a theoretical entity that occupies a space in the vicinity of our chest cavity. It's a positive, purposeful force and it's at the core of our being. It's the part of us that loves without restriction and accepts without judgment. If we want to know our soul, the first step is to recognize that we have a soul by whatever name we may call it. The next step is to allow ourselves to consider if I have a soul, if I have this something that is me, what is my soul? What does my soul want? What is the relationship between my soul and the other thing that I call me? How does my soul affect my life? When the energy of the soul is recognized and acknowledge and valued, then it begins to infuse the life of the personality.

When our personality begins to adequately serve the energy of the soul, then that's authentic empowerment. That is the goal in which we are involved and that is the reason for our being. Every experience that we have, and will have, encourages the alignment of our personality with our soul. Every circumstance and situation gives us the opportunity to chose this path, to bring into the world through our unending, unfathomable reverence for and love of life, our soul, that it can shine through us.

We're all growing our souls. That's why we're here. And it's not always easy or smooth. It requires our time and our attention, our honesty and our self-respect. And it requires our love and our hope and our faith. Our belief that we do not have to be locked into old destructive patterns, that we and all human beings can learn, and can grow, and can change. Can and will. And as we grow our souls day by day, we are helping other souls to grow. We're helping the world, the whole interdependent web of all existence, to grow in compassion and justice and grace. May this our spiritual community always be a place where we sing together the song of the soul. And may our song go forth into the world that all may sing with us.

DARKNESS

This is a service In Praise of Darkness. May our gathering invoke the spirit of life which is present in darkness, on our darkest times of rest, love, joy and pain.

Liberal religion, in fact, our American way of life is often considered to have been born in the period of history in the 18th century known as the Enlightenment. Now the enlightenment is usually thought of as a great positive step forward by humankind. It marks a turning point in human thinking, a shift of emphasis from mystery to reason, from myth to fact, from fate to progress. Life became a series of questions to be answered and problems to be solved. Science and technology developed and flourished and became the central focus of much of Western civilization.

And as technology flourished we became, literally, en-lightened. The invention of the light bulb, the harnessing of electric power had a powerful and profound effect on the way we live our lives. We moved from being a primarily agrarian society, living in tune with the rhythms of day and night, dark and light, and the seasons of the year, to an increasingly industrialized and urbanized society with the ability to light our lives 24 hours a day. And now not only do we have light bulbs and neon lights but we have a new kind of a light machine you might say, the television. Our light inventions become ever more seductive and ever more demanding.

We rarely experience true darkness anymore. Even at midnight, especially around here, the sky glows with the reflection of city lights. We sleep with night lights or the glow of the street lights. For many people, darkness has come to seem unnatural- alien- perhaps even frightening. If we are afraid of darkness, of course, we have good reason these days. The possibility of becoming a victim of crime is a real danger. But it's more than that. We've come to see darkness as a lack of light, and we don't like to lack anything.

When it's dark, something is missing. We can't see clearly. And we have been accustomed to seeing clearly, to looking at something all the time, something external, all the time. We are uneasy, fearful, bored by imagelessness. As a corollary, perhaps, we also fear and avoid silence. And our souls, our spirits, pay the price. Lives, spirits, psyches, that are totally light oriented are superficial, because they lack the deep dark roots that nourish and surprise and ground us.

When we take our nourishment only from electric lights and electronic images, from words and pictures commercially produced, our creative and spiritual growth is stunted. Even when our focus is on our own words and pictures, we need the contrast, the balance, of darkness and stillness and quiet. Much of Western religion has become very light oriented. Darkness is equated with sin and evil; light with goodness and salvation. We talk about people seeing the light or coming into the light or carrying the light within, but we don't talk much about dreaming in the dark, or even praying. Darkness is to be overcome, vanquished; gotten rid of, escaped. And it's strange, really, that this should be so.

And our bodies, at least, know darkness as a friend. For example, we very likely began in the dark, conceived in dark nights of love making, what Matthew Fox calls the dark sacrament of love and intimacy and sensuality. And we spent the first nine months of our fetal development in the womb, which was dark but sheltering, not fearful. And our heart, our liver, our intestines, our brain, all those things the kids like to hear about, all the beautiful and harmonious and working parts of our bodies, go about their business, night and day, completely in the dark. Strange, we often equate death with darkness, yet in darkness life begins and flourishes.

The sun doesn't penetrate all of space. Much of space is dark. Much of the birth of the cosmos itself was done in the dark- just as ours was. The sun has not always existed. First there was darkness. It seems so vast, the darkness of space. Maybe that's what frightens us.

The seed growing underground is growing in the dark just as the fetus grows in the mother's womb. This image of darkness seems so close, so intimate. Maybe that's what frightens us.

These are our origins, the origins of life; dark, silent, wonderful, fearful, and our awareness and celebrating of these origins, of the wonder and the fear, can help us get in touch with our spiritual depths. When I was an artist a long time ago, a painter, one of the things that intrigued me most was negative space, the space around and between things. I could draw or paint the spaces and of course when I did that I also defined the objects, and made them appear. As an art teacher I often had my students work this way, paint or draw only what wasn't there. They were always amazed and fascinated by the results. Try it yourself sometime. Draw all the spaces around and between all the parts of a chair, or a tree, or your hand and see how beautiful and how positive and how powerful the negative can be.

Most of us have been trained and conditioned to see life in terms of dualism. And in this way of doing things, the positive is good, the negative is bad and they are poles apart. I prefer the Taoist image of life, an unending circle, half dark, half light each half containing some of the other, light in the darkness, darkness in the light. Positive contained in the negative, negative in the positive.

Darkness is uncluttered space, and oh how we need that. We go along clutching and hanging on to so much stuff, so much hurt and anger and pain from the past, so much fear and doubt and insecurity. So many outworn images and roles and behaviors that we don't need anymore. Why is it so hard to let go? And we hold on to old dreams, old ideas, old loves and hates, long past the time when they could ever have any reality in our lives. But still we hang on. Why can't we let them go? Well, habit for one thing. It just seems easier in the short run to hang on than to try to change. And fear, for another thing. Fear that if we let go of something, it will leave a hole in our lives. A deep, dark hole. Or fear that if we let go of one thing, it will start a chain reaction and we'll lose it all. Or fear, maybe, that we'll lose control. Or fear that we'll have to face whatever it is before we can let it go.

Letting go means that we learn not to cling so tightly. Cling so tightly to our egos. Not to cling so tightly to the goods and the goals of our consumer society. So tightly that we are defined by them, and caged by them. We learn to let be, ourselves, others and life itself. And not be so dissatisfied of being ourselves. Not so dissatisfied that we project onto others our attitudes, our fears, our disappointments or our guilt. Letting go means allowing pain to be pain.

As human beings, we are created to experience both joy and sorrow. Not joy or sorrow. Pleasure and pain,. Not pleasure or pain. We will know sickness and health. Not sickness or health. And it is all these things together that make us fully human and that give our lives richness and meaning. Probably most of us here today are living with some degree of pain, physical pain, emotional pain or psychological pain. Pain has been called the Dark Night of the Soul and we don't want it. We fear it, we deny it, we push it away. We feel weak, guilty and angry. Accepting pain is never easy. But if we deny it, we deny our humanness. Where just as joy and fulfillment help us find meaning for our lives, so do pain and loss.

We accept pain, because it helps us to understand others. It connects us to others. All social action, all striving to overcome evils of racism, sexism, ageism, of oppression and repression, all our struggles for freedom and justice are born of our shared pain. That is the dark mystery of pain. It binds us together, all members of the human family. We are not meant to be happy and cheerful all of the time. We are not meant to spend every moment of our lives in high gear, doing, accomplishing, achieving, acquiring, running. Without the peaceful darkness of sleep and dreams, our daylight lives would become crazed and desperate. We need time to rest, to contemplate. We need time to meditate. Time to look within, into the depths of our souls. The human race, says Matthew Fox, cannot continue to flee the darkness, and embrace an enlightenment which doesn't include an endarkenment.

Together we can create places, safe places, this place, where we can share and celebrate the totality of mystery and wonder in our lives, joy and sorrow, pleasure and pain, silence and song. And all the wide range of feelings and experiences that lie in between. So let us affirm the beauty and the worth of darkness as well as light, in the human soul and in the human face. Then we shall make real our dream of unity in diversity within each and among all.

My this be so.

IN THE NAME OF GOD
EXPLORATION AND EXPLOITATION OF
THE NEW WORLD

In a museum in Havana there are two skulls of Christopher Columbus, one when he was a boy and one when he was a man.

Mark Twain

In fourteen hundred and ninety two, Columbus sailed the ocean blue.... How many of you can remember saying, singing, chanting that as a child? All United States school children know about Columbus. And we all know the same story. It went something like this: From the beginning of time until 1492, most people thought the world was flat, that if you got into a ship and sailed far enough out on the ocean, you would come to the edge of the world, and maybe, if you couldn't turn around in time, you'd just fall off. A sailor named Christopher Columbus didn't believe that. He believed that the world was round, which meant that if you traveled long enough and far enough in the same direction, you'd come back to where you started.

Columbus wanted to try it! He wanted to try it because he thought this would be a good, easier way to get to India, where he could get spices and other goods to trade, and he would get rich. He also wanted to find out if he was right and what would happen. So Columbus tried to raise money for the voyage. For this he needed a sponsor. It wasn't easy. He went to Queen Isabella of Spain. She and her husband, King Ferdinand, finally decided to be Columbus' sponsors. He got three ships and we all know the names: the *Nina*, the *Pinta* and the *Santa Maria*, and off he sailed to find India. Of course, instead he found something much more wonderful and important. He discovered America. There was more to the story but this was the part everyone knew and remembered.

But what happened next? What happened after Columbus "discovered" America? The modern version of the story is not so pretty.

Columbus was convinced he'd found the East Indies, and would claim great riches for Spain and for himself. After exploring the nearby islands he returned to Spain in triumph. He made a second voyage in 1493 and explored Hispaniola, Cuba, Jamaica and the Venezuelan coast. Then he returned to Spain in 1496 to justify his exploration. His prophecies and promises had not come true; there had been none of the expected riches of the orient. He returned on his third voyage in 1498. But in 1500 Spain sent a governor to the new world. He had Columbus arrested and sent back to Spain in chains. Columbus did well enough, though, to finance one last voyage. He died in 1506 in Spain, neglected and poverty stricken, but still convinced he'd discovered the Western route to the East.

Although the first Spanish colonies were disappointing in their lack of rich resources, it was suspected that there was greater wealth inland. Indeed, that was so. In 1519, the governor of Cuba sent a fleet under Hernan Cortez to explore and settle inland areas. This part of the story becomes more familiar. Cortez founded the settlement of Veracruz and took over the Aztec capital (now Mexico City). Its ruler, Montezuma, welcomed him and was promptly imprisoned by Cortez.

Next came Pizarro, who continued Spanish conquest and exploitation. The Inca empire was subjugated. And so it continued. Spanish colonization profoundly affected the area and the people. Introduction of European crops and live stock destroyed the native domestic life and altered the ecological balance. The destruction of Aztec society resulted in an alienated, enfeebled native population that easily succumbed to European disease.

Latin America became a mixed culture dominated by the culture of the Spanish settlers. The highly developed civilizations of the Aztecs and Incas totally disappeared. The tribes that survived were the least developed, because they were the least threatening or the least worth bothering with. The pattern was set for centuries to come; the domination of the Spanish culture and religion and the subjugation and oppression of the indigenous population.

The Christian conquerors seemed to have few qualms about what they did. They believed that they had the right to take the land and resources and destroy the people. As Christians, they were taught and they believed that these non-Christian, heathen beings were less than human. They measured these people by their own cultural standards, and for the Spanish conquerors, there was no contest. The natives, the Indians, were clearly inferior, with outlandish customs and pagan rituals and ignorance of proper speech, education, morals and law.

There was great debate, however, as to whether the Indians (as they had been named by the Spaniards) had souls or whether they were animals. It was finally decided that though they were clearly and permanently inferior, they did have souls and therefore must be converted to Christianity as quickly as possible, and forcibly if necessary.

This view prevailed throughout the White, male European conquest- settling of all the North America as well. The three goals of the Christian invaders in dealing with all of these indigenous people, north and south, were evangelization, pacification and enculturation of these pagan savages. It seems never to have occurred to the conquerors that the indigenous cultures had any worth; that their religious, spiritual and social values were worth any effort toward understanding, let alone appreciating or, heaven forbid, emulating. Superior and inferior status was never in question, from the day Columbus and his crew touched shore through the exploration, colonization and industrialization of all of North America, and the resulting evangelization of the indigenous population by the church. This evangelization process was seen as necessary, right and inevitable. It was first carried out by three different Christian missions: Southwestern, with Spanish missions and Northeastern, with French and English missions. The Franciscans were in charge of the Spanish missions, the Jesuits in the French missions and the Puritans started the English missions.

It seems that there was never any thought on the part of these Christian missionaries/invaders/conquerors that Native American and European religions and cultures might coexist; might live side by side in the huge expanse that was now named America. The whole thrust. from the beginning, was conquest. Yes, adventure and exploration were part of the picture, part of the progress, but they were to result in conquest, control and profit.

And as we look at the unfolding story of European occupation of the New World, we can certainly see the tremendously important role played by the church. We see the power that religion has in shaping culture and society. The story of what happened in the new world, in America, is just one example which can help us to realize what has happened many times, in many places, throughout human history, the disrespect, denial and destruction of one culture by another.

The cultural differences between the native Americans and the invaders were many and profound. The Christian invaders were, first of all, monotheistic. Native Americans, by contrast, believed that many Gods, divine beings, were needed to make the world's components run smoothly. They gave the earth respected status of its own and so they could neither share nor understand the European belief that the natural world was simply an economic resource.

Secondly, the Christian doctrine of salvation contrasted strongly with the Native American's ideas about personal identity. Christians saw themselves as a separate and distinct group of people, saved and claimed by a merciful and personal God, but only through each individual's personal belief and morality, each person's individual responsibility. There were no such ideas in Native American life. There, everyone belonged to the group and would return after death to the spirit world regardless of personal virtue or demerits. There was no ultimate life of pleasure for the good and punishment for the wicked.

Differing ideas of moral obligation were another area of conflict. The Christians believed that their ethical guidelines derived from biblical and theological traditions; sources that transcended history. Native Americans, by contrast, derived their sense of duty from the local community and its needs. In other words, for Christians, authority came from sacred scripture and church law. For Native Americans, authority lay in the community itself.

Human sinfulness and the need for salvation were probably the most important areas where Christians and Native Americans found no common ground, the same areas in which Unitarians and Universalists parted company from Orthodox Christianity. Native Americans distinguished between good and bad conduct in their communities. But they did not have the concept of universal guilt; of a fundamental inadequacy in human nature. They viewed sin as a limited circumstantial act; a social mistake for which they could atone with material gifts. Misdemeanor required compensation rather than punishment. They rarely agreed that anyone should die for a serious crime. Consequently, it made no sense for anyone to die for his sinfulness. Accustomed to property compensation, they did not value blood sacrifice, not even the death of Jesus, because in their culture such sacrifices were only exacted from enemies. The story of Christ's atoning death seemed to them inappropriate and unnecessary. In keeping with their dim view of predestination, the New England Puritans emphasized the depravity of human nature and the need for divine grace. Native Americans did not perceive human life as congenitally wicked.

Despite these many contrasting views of religion, human nature and theology, the Christian invaders prevailed. They were so convinced that they were right that they simply assumed that their religion and culture were destined by Divine Providence to dominate the land. And they were right, or so it seemed. Their goal was to teach or coerce the Native Americans to lead a Christian life. Convinced that Native American culture and religion and the way they were expressed were totally wrong, the Christian missionaries confiscated religious objects used in the despised, pagan, savage rituals. They buried the sacred masks, instruments and prayer sticks. In their religious conviction and zeal, they helped destroy the native culture and never realized or accepted the cruelty and tragedy of what they had done.

Only now are their descendants, those of us who are of White European ancestry, beginning to understand the extent of the harm that was done in the name of religion, culture, progress and morality. Only now are we all beginning to realize the extent to which this country has been shaped, misshaped, by the blind myths of cultural superiority.

Only now have we begun to seek, explore and reclaim that which was lost or stolen or perverted or imprisoned. Only now are we beginning to understand the damage, the trauma that has been inflicted on the interdependent web of existence of which we , all, every living thing, are a part. Only now are we beginning to search for new myths, new heroes, new models and stories that will include rather than exclude; open us to one another rather than wall us apart; encourage the flourishing of true individualism rather than a narrow particularism.

Only now are we perhaps beginning to understand what true religion can and should be about. Religion that will find ways to express and celebrate all our wonderful human diversity. Religion that will discover and celebrate the human unity that lies in the heart of it all; waiting, waiting, century after century, waiting for each of us to understand, to finally begin to know how to live together, in peace, in wholeness, in the holy union that may yet be known, in and through us.

Spirit of Life, present in each yet greater than all, may it be so.

REFLECTIONS ON HOME AND HUNGER

Home...where people love you and are overjoyed to see you when you've been away. Isn't that what we all want? Even when we've behaved foolishly, irrationally, or wrongly, we want to know there's always a place where we are welcome, where we are safe. When life is stormy , when adventure turns into misadventure, when we can't find our way, we want to know we can go home. *Home.*

It seems so right, doesn't it. It seems so right. We each need a loving, accepting, safe home. We don't need a castle, a mansion; we don't need House Beautiful. Just a loving, accepting safe home, nothing fancy. And if that's what we all need, that's what we all should have, right? Wrong.

Our title for this morning is entitled "Reflections on Home and Hunger." It was inspired in part by our mission in the coming week of serving at the Homeless Family Shelter. We have volunteered to work and serve dinner each night to about five homeless families, mostly mothers and children, and to stay there in the shelter with them all night. In doing this we see, face to face, the most basic issues about home, and hunger, the need for shelter and for food. Survival needs. Shelter from the weather and from violence. Food for hungry bellies. Shelter for people who have no homes. Food for people who have no place to cook. No pots and pans. No groceries.

Most of us will never experience this level of need. Some may. We are all aware of how hunger and homelessness are a growing problem, a growing manifestation of economic injustice. Need at this level calls on us for charity. We fortunate human beings must help our less fortunate sisters and brothers. This is a basic religious teaching, an obligation of many if not all faiths. Our Unitarian Universalist stance is illustrated in the Readings in our Hymn Book:

Isaiah—If you offer your food to the hungry and satisfy the afflicted, you shall be like a watered garden, like a spring whose waters never fail.

Buddhism- Just as a mother, with her own life, protects her only child from hurt, so within yourself foster a limitless concern for every living creature.

Islam—To worship God is nothing other than to serve the people. If fate brings suffering to one member, the others cannot stay at rest.

Taoism—When all the people of the world love, then the strong will not overpower the weak, the many will not oppress the few, the wealthy will not mock the poor, the honored will not disdain the humble, and the cunning will not deceive the simple.

Christianity: Matthew 25—I was hungry and you gave me food, I was thirsty and you gave me drink, I was a stranger and you welcomed me, I was naked and you clothed me, I was sick and you visited me, I was in prison and you came to me. Whatever you did for the least of my brothers and sisters, you did for me.

James 2—What good is it my brothers and sisters if you say you have faith but do not have works? Can faith save you? If a brother or sister is naked and lacks daily food and one of you says to them: "Go in peace, keep warm and eat your fill," and yet you do not supply their bodily needs, what is the good of that? So faith by itself, if it has no works, is dead. Show me your faith apart from your works and I by my works, will show you my faith.

And so we put our faith to work. Our faith in the worth and dignity of every person, our faith that each has a place in the interdependent web of all existence, and we reach out to those in need. But, as we know, there is more to life than just survival. A shelter in a church basement is not home. A meal served by volunteers does not assuage the hunger of the heart,of the spirit.

And so we must not only practice charity and give what is needed; we must also work to change the conditions that promote and maintain poverty and injustice, homelessness and hunger.

We also know that we may have a house yet still not have a home. We may have a kitchen full, a table full of food yet still be hungry. We have described a *home* as the place where people love you and are overjoyed to see you when you've been away. And we can describe *hunger* as the yearning to be fulfilled, as well as have a full stomach. Religion speaks to these needs, too. The needs of faith and hope as well as charity. Think of the songs, hymns, sung by the African American slaves and still sung today. Hymns that held out the hope, the faith, the promise of freedom, of crossing over to a new place, out of the slavery and oppression of this life and into eternal life, of the hunger to go home to the freedom land; freedom of body and soul.

Yes, religion through the ages has spoken to the human need, human hunger, for spiritual fulfillment, the hunger to be home in the world and the universe. Certainly Unitarian Universalism has always spoken of that hunger for home. And our focus has been on this world rather than the next, on creating heaven on earth, or at least in working to create a better and more universally accessible way of life for all.

We in this congregation have come from many different religious traditions. We've come from many different kinds of homes as well, some from joyful, loving, secure homes and some, perhaps, and unfortunately, not much like that at all. In any case, we know that's what we want, what we hunger for, for ourselves and our children.

I would guess, from what I know and am learning about you, that you are quite exceptional in creating homes where people love one another and are happy to see one another. You bring that spirit, that willingness to welcome, affirm and love, with you and your children, into this congregation and into the larger world. You have respect and compassion for the hard hunger pains of those in need, and you are in touch with your own hunger, a good hunger, to love and be loved; a hunger for connectedness, for learning and growing together, a hunger for the unity and diversity which enriches and expands our lives.

You have come together here, with your hunger, your dreams and vision, your many talents, your enthusiasm, your energy. And you are creating a home, the Unitarian Universalist Society of the Palisades, a place where people love one another and are happy to see one another. Yes! I know that's true. And as I've told you many times, as I stand here, where I can see all your faces, I see that love, I see that responsiveness, that is so beautiful, so present, so alive, that I am actually thrilled, touched, by the strength of the Spirit of Life and Love, the spirit of God moving among us.

And I know that I am home, here, with you. We are going to go through many changes in the months and years ahead, as we grow in numbers, in connectedness, in our ability to reach out to others, to make a difference. We will move, we will build, a larger home, a larger community, a larger life together. We will BE a home for one another and for all who come to us.

COMMON THREAD

One of our most cherished Unitarian Universalist Principles affirms respect for the interdependent web of all existence of which we are a part. When I think of the web I see a huge, perhaps infinite tapestry. Complex, multi-colored and textured, and each life is a thread nearly invisible in the larger work. Yet each thread is uniquely spun, itself multi- colored and multi-textured. And these invisible threads generate, the magnitude and the complexity of the overall design; each thread is necessary to the creation of that tapestry.

This is my vision, a vision which led me to my call to ministry, and which empowered me to answer that call, which underlies my commitment to this congregation and to our shared vision of unity in diversity. Each of us, each person, a unique and beautiful thread, essential to the tapestry of life. We are what is called the weft of the tapestry. But beautiful and unique as each of our threads may be, we can not weave that tapestry alone. We would be no more than a tangled knot, if we didn't have the warp thread to hold our tapestry together.

Now the warp thread is the thread which strings the loom, and it's not uniquely colored or textured, it's plain. Usually a neutral, natural undyed color, and it's very strong and very even. And it's dependable, too. It will not break. It holds steady all our colorful strands to weave over and under, and over and under, weave a beautiful, intricate pattern that obscures that warp thread. A pattern that covers the warp thread, that makes it invisible. But the warp thread is always there, holding it all together. The basis on which all that beauty, and all that complexity, can fasten. That is the common thread that we celebrate this morning.

I envision this as a 3-ply thread, made of love, and respect, and responsibility. Now I could simply call this common thread love, and I'm tempted to do just that. Love is the binding force that holds it all together, that holds us all together. Love is the heart and the soul of the mystery of life. Love is the key to our survival. Our individual spiritual survival, and our collective survival as well. In a simple and yet profound statement, God is Love, we acknowledge the power and the possibility and the totality of love.

And yet, and yet, in human terms, I think we need to name, to lift up, respect and responsibility, as inextricably, intertwined in that thread of love. Because love, the word love, has become so trivialized in our culture, that we are in danger of losing touch with its power and with its truth. We love ice cream, or tennis, or L.A. Law. We love murder mysteries, Volvos or bagels. We love our new coat, or we love our old coat. We love, we love. Have you ever noticed how much easier it is to say I love chocolate, or moo goo gai pan, or whatever, rather than just say, I love you. How much easier it is sometimes, quite frankly, to feel more love for chocolate than for that other person, because loving people is not easy.

When it comes to people we have some very romantic ideas about love. We equate love with adoration sometimes, or admiration, or pleasure, or reciprocity, or sentiment, sexuality, happiness, companionship, the list goes on and on. So does love. It goes on past all those things. Love is the warp on which we weave life. And if we can truly touch and interact with and know that thread, that strong string of love, then we can create patterns of great beauty, and power, and meaning, patterns of justice and compassion. We can create whole cloth.

And I would hope that thinking and talking about respect and responsibility, will help us get past the romanticism, past the sentiment, past that Blue Bird of Happiness, to love as the essential truth of our existence. Remember that Aretha Franklin song. I loved it. yes I did. "R-E-S-P-E-C-T," all I really want is a little respect. When we love with respect we honor the essential worth and dignity of each person, including ourselves. This is our first Unitarian Universalist principle. We will probably all agree that it's a good one. I would say that each of us tries to live with respect, and on the whole I'd say we're doing pretty well.

On the whole. It's the details though, that sometimes get in the way. Respect means paying attention, really being present to the other person, or to ourselves. Letting go of all the distractions and worries and business, and allowing the time and the space for real relationship, real connectedness, to happen. Listening, and really hearing. Speaking from the heart. Sharing words, and sharing silences. Staying with the struggle to communicate and to understand. Acknowledging that this is important, vital. Not to change the other person. Not to convert, not to convince, not to overwhelm. To offer and share our truths, our realities, our hopes and our dreams. To find that unity beneath our diversities. That is love, with respect.

And with this, of course, comes responsibility. More and more technology has forced us to learn that we never act in isolation. When we tug upon one thread of that tapestry of the web, everything changes. Scott Peck has defined love as caring for the other's spiritual well being as we do our own. And spiritual well being cannot be separated from the totality of the person.. As Unitarian Universalists we don't believe that we can hand someone a stone, or an empty bowl, and then pray for their soul. Once we have seen each other, once we have met each other, in our struggle and in our vulnerability, we cannot simply turn away. We must reach out our hands, affirm and strengthen that thread that unites us and binds us together. We reach out on the largest and most global scale possible right down to the most intimate. I would guess that each of us has a pretty well developed sense of social responsibility. We care about world hunger, and oppression and economic and racial injustice. We vote, we give our money and time to worthy causes. We try to be informed and learn about the issues. We do more than wring our hands or shake our heads. We network, because we know we can't do it alone. But our compassion, our caring for the world at large is learned and strengthened through the personal contacts and relationships that we make in our daily lives.

My mother was my earliest and strongest influence. She taught me to hate racism and anti-semitism, and all forms of bigotry and prejudice. I grew up feeling very, very strongly about these things. As an adult, I did, or I thought I did, what I could. I stood up for what I believed in, I spoke out. I worked for fair housing. I was fervently committed to the civil rights movement. But I lived in a white world. And then, as some of you know because I've told this story, I went to New York Theological Seminary. A school dedicated to Urban Ministry, where the majority of students were African American, with many who were African, Hispanic and Asian, and with some who were White. We studied and we worked together for a very intense three years. We explored our traditions, our theologies, our ethics, our feelings, our fears. And my theories and beliefs and commitments were tested and challenged and affirmed. They were made real in that shared life. Many of us were, I believe, transformed, as I was. We confronted and shared and struggled to understand our great diversity. And we found and affirmed in the process, our underlying unity. That's how it happened, one on one. And what we learned moves with us into the larger world.

Most of us have had such experience, and that's why we're building this congregation. We share the vision of a safe place, where people, adults and children, of diverse racial, ethnic, cultural and economic groups, gay, straight, older, younger, of varying abilities and disabilities, all those people, can come together and learn from and about each other. Can become transformed in the process. And can, in turn, transform the world. Grandiose? No! This is how things really happen. I believe it, and I think that you do, too. And I'll tell you, and you'll tell me, it's not easy. Because if we are serious about this, it means we have to work at it.

Whitney Young, (a Unitarian Universalist and former head of the Urban League) and many others, remarked that eleven o'clock on Sunday morning is the most segregated hour in America. He was talking about race, but we can extend it to other forms of diversity as well. We want it to be different for our children. We want it to be different for ourselves and for others. And so we are working to create a Sunday morning, and the rest of the week too, that is not segregated, that is integrated in the deepest and most profound sense.

That means, what does it mean? It means that we have to teach Sunday School. It means that we have to work on the membership, and the finance, and the program and the social responsibility committees.. It means that we have to raise and give money. It means that we have to make the coffee. Because it we don't, who will? If we don't follow our dream of Unity in Diversity, and build a place of love and respect and responsibility, who will? We're pioneers. Maybe you didn't set out to be a pioneer. But if you're here, that's what you are! And I commend you. I welcome you and I love you. I want to talk the talk with you. I want to walk the walk with you. I want to learn how to do it better. And I never want to do it, alone.

I want to read something for you. Something that you probably heard many times. But somehow it's taken on new meaning to me:

> If I have prophetic powers and understand all mysteries and knowledge. And if I have faith so as to move mountains, but do not have love, I am nothing. If I give away all my possessions and if I hand over my body to be burned, but do not have love, I gain nothing. Love is patient, love is kind, love is not envious or boastful, arrogant or rude. It does not insist on its own way. It is not irritable or resentful. It does not rejoice in wrongdoing, but rejoices in the truth. It bares all things, believes all things, hopes all things, endures all things. Love never ends. Prophecies will come to an end. Tongues will cease. Knowledge will come to an end. We know in part. We prophecy in part. But when the complete comes, the partial will come to an end. When I was a child, I spoke like a child. I thought like a child. I reasoned like a child. When I became an adult I put an end to childish ways. Now we see in a mirror, in a riddle. Then we will see face to face. Now I know in part. Then, I will know fully. Now faith, hope and love abide, these three, and the greatest of these is love.
>
> Corinthians 1:13

ASHES TO ASHES, DUST TO DUST

W ell, it's almost Lent. It begins this Wednesday. How many of you grew up in a family or church that observed Lent? I did. And it started with Ash Wednesday, when we all went to church, went up and knelt at the altar rail at St. Francis of Assisi Roman Catholic church, and the priest dipped his thumb in a bowl of ashes and made a cross on each person's forehead and said, in Latin, "Remember, man that thou art dust and into dust thou shall return." He said *Man*, but we all knew he meant everybody. Actually, since he said it in Latin, and really fast too, it didn't really mean very much. It was just something you had to do because you were Catholic.

And then you went around all day with a black thumb print on your forehead so everybody knew you were Catholic, and a good Catholic because you did what you were supposed to do. There were more things we were supposed to do during Lent, too. We were supposed to fast and we were supposed to give up at least one thing we didn't want to give up. At least that's the way I understood it.

The nuns would talk about this in Religious Instructions. They'd tell us how Lent was a time for penance and how the various saints had fasted for days and weeks or how they wore hair shirts or lived with only the barest essentials, and spent their lives praying, never playing. Most or this sounded pretty weird, grim. And I didn't remember any of us ever wanting to become saints. Saints suffered to a degree beyond anything we could relate to. But giving up something, just for Lent, that was a fairly universal practice in my community. Like making New Years resolutions. Adults gave up smoking. Or drinking. Or playing cards. My mother says a lot of the women offered to give up sex. (This was the pre-pill generation) They practiced the rhythm method, and you know what they called people who practiced rhythm. *Parents!*

Well, anyhow. Back to Lent. Children and adults gave up candy. That seemed to be the big Lenten sacrifice for kids. NO candy. You could also give up chewing gum or going to the movies. I think that was about it. Now here is where I was really different. Maybe it was the true beginnings of my Unitarian Universalism. I was a skinny child in the days when children were not supposed to be skinny. My parents use to try to get me to eat candy, and more candy than I wanted. So when Lent came, they didn't want me to give up candy, or any food. And since I didn't smoke or drink or even go to the movies very often, I grew up not making the usual children's Lenten sacrifices. And when I became an adult, I became a Unitarian Universalist. And I never heard much about Lent again.

But you know, lately I've become curious. Just what was, is, Lent all about, anyhow? Is there any meaning there for me? For us? Any insight we can gain about ourselves? Humanity? Religion? History? I ask these questions perhaps a bit more than I used to. It seems as if others are asking those questions too, in science and medicine and in the many fields related to the study of human culture, human being.

We're discovering, for example, that many of the old folk remedies really work. That many so-called old wives tales contain much practical wisdom from which we can learn and benefit today. That medicines synthesized in laboratories aren't necessarily better than old tried-and-true basics. That many plants, known or not yet discovered, have curative powers if we but take the time and open mindedness necessary to discover them. We're discovering that primitive doesn't mean less intelligent or less human or less civilized. We're discovering the richness and complexity of ancient cultures; of different cultures.

We're discovering that we, twentieth century human beings, with our science and technology are not the crowning glory, the final achievement, the ultimate goal, of creation or evolution or the workings of the cosmos or the mind of God. We're just us, trying to survive, to make it, in our world today, as every generation before us has tried to do.

And so just as the scientist is taking another look at grandma's pithy sayings and home remedies, so I, as a minister, am looking at Judeo-Christian traditions. Not because I want to adopt them or reclaim them, but because I've learned that they can give me a fuller understanding of human history and human nature, and perhaps point out for me some questions, needs and struggles that are common to every age, every generation.

And so, what about Lent? First, a few facts which I've found interesting: I grew up knowing that Lent was a period of 40 days, beginning with Ash Wednesday and culminating in Easter Sunday. I never paid much attention to how the dates for this period were decided, though I suppose I was told. For those who don't know or don't remember, Easter is what is called a movable feast. That's why we have to check the new calendar to see what the date will be. Easter falls on the date of the first full moon after the vernal equinox, which this year is on March 20th, since Lent is 40 days in length. So Ash Wednesday is 40 days before Easter, right?

Wrong. Sundays don't count. Sundays, in the Christian church, aren't fast days because they commemorate the first Easter. So Ash Wednesday is 40 days plus Sundays, or 46 days before the Sunday following the first full moon after the Vernal Equinox. Now I know why I never really understood all this. It was, and is, just easier to look at the calendar.

Why 40 days for Lent? The most common belief is that it commemorates the 40 days that Jesus is said to have fasted in the desert after his baptism and before the beginning of his public ministry. The number 40 has long had a symbolic importance in the Hebrew Bible, or OT, as well. Moses spent 40 days in the wilderness, so did Elijah. The Jews wandered 40 years searching for the Promised Land. Jonah gave the city of Ninevah 40 days in which to repent. Lent was originally 40 hours rather than 40 days. It was a period of strict fasting in preparation for the celebration of Easter.

Soon, it became the custom to baptize new Christians on Easter Eve, and the period of fasting and preparation for baptism was extended to 40 days. Eventually this period was decreed to be observed by all Christians. And in time, the focus of Lent changed from a time of preparation to a time of penitence. During the middle ages, sinners were accepted back into the church only after doing public penance during Lent.

Yes, just as Christmas grew out of ancient celebrations of the winter solstice, so did Lent and Easter also have roots in ancient myths and celebrations. The word Lent is said to come from the Anglo-Saxon word lenten, meaning Spring, and the German Lenz, meaning the time when the days lengthen. Humans have always been concerned with the mysteries of life and death, and the winter solstice and the coming of Spring are the times that bring these mysteries closest to human consciousness.

Humans have probably always struggled to give meaning and purpose to life and death. They have probably always struggled with their need for control. And so the image of God would be of the one who had supreme control. Humans, however, tried to at least influence God through penance and petition and obedience to God's laws as interpreted by the church. According to church law, unforgiven sinners went to Hell, eternal death and damnation. Forgiven sinners could go to Heaven, eternal life. So Lent, as a time to do penance and seek forgiveness, was a way to bring people to God and to the church.

Perhaps there are still many people who take Lent seriously as a time of repentance. Except for some of my ministerial colleagues from the traditional Christian churches, though, I don't know many who see Lent that way. For most, I think it's symbolic, part of the tradition of the church to which they belong. Penitence has for the most part become synonymous with guilt, and guilt is rather a dirty word for people of this generation.

And yet, as people in 12 Step programs know, and as more and more of us are discovering, or realizing, penitence, acknowledging the negative or harmful things we have done, to ourselves and others, and getting in touch with our feelings of shame or guilt or discomfort or disconnectedness that result from our negative behavior, and getting in touch, too, with the yearning to do better and our need to make amends, penitence, the ability to say: "I did wrong. I'm sorry. How can I make amends? I want to do better." This kind of penitence is something we all need.

We've talked here before about Unitarianism and Universalism developing as religious responses to doctrines that proclaimed humans as sinful, fallen creatures, who could never be saved by their own efforts, doomed and damned by God's all powerful decree and saved only through faith in Jesus Christ as Lord and Savior. The Unitarians said NO. Humans are not born depraved, fallen sinners. Humans are born with free will, capable of choosing the good, capable through education, culture and religion of learning and growing and aspiring to ideals of truth, beauty, love and justice. Yes, humans can do terrible things, too. And so it is our human purpose and task to help each other develop spiritually and choose the good.

Universalists said, in reaction to the harsh doctrine of human sinfulness and depravity, and their punishment by hellfire and damnation: NO! Humans are not born destined for hell. God is a God of Love, not cruelty or vengeance or punishment. The Supreme Creator is all loving and all humans may be saved by that love. So does this mean that the Calvinists, or others who believe in the doctrine of original sin, need Lent but we Unitarian Universalists don't? That seems to be the general feeling.

And I certainly agree that we don't need church law telling us that now we must repent because it's that time of year the 40 days, not counting Sundays after the first full moon after the vernal equinox. And I don't think we need a thumb print cross smeared on our foreheads with ashes made from burning last years Sunday palms. I don't mean to devalue these rituals. They have great meaning and power and symbolism for many people. However, probably most of us are here today because we do not choose this way as our spiritual path.

Yet our human need for penitence, forgiveness and atonement, I call it at-one-ment, remains. And I am coming more and more to believe that we have need for communal expression of this human need. I firmly believe in our human freedom to choose good and in our human need to help each other to make those positive choices. And I believe that the Spirit of Life, of Love, of Creation, present in each yet greater than all, that spirit which may be called God, can never be a spirit of damnation or cruelty or vengeance or vindication.

But I also believe that our freedom to choose means that we can choose evil as well as good. It means that we must know there is good, must experience good, in order to be able to choose it. It means that because we have choice we will sometimes choose selfishly, carelessly, unwisely. We will cause hurt, and will need, all through our lives, to face and deal with our wrong doing, our SINS, and to find ways to learn and go forward rather than sink into guilt, apathy or despair.

In other words, I believe that all our lives we will struggle to love ourselves and others more fully and to live our lives as expressions of that love. We can't do this by ourselves. And that, basically, is why we are here, why we get up and come here on Sunday morning when we could be sleeping or reading the paper or doing any number of other pleasant, Sunday morning-ish things. We are here because of our need and our struggle to lead loving lives. Sounds simple, doesn't it? And yet we know how complicated it really is.

In coming here we acknowledge this, and we acknowledge our hope that we, in associating with one another, in singing together and sharing our thoughts, our questions, our joys and concerns, in struggling to challenge and trust and care for each other, that we will indeed help each other learn the ways of love.

We know, because we are human, we cannot lead charmed lives. Each one of us here today will have our share of trouble and sorrow and pain. We will also know joy and accomplishment and fulfillment. We will all, at some time, be selfish and thoughtless or greedy or mean or envious or lazy or destructive. Things won't go right and we'll want to blame someone. We'll fear that really it's all our fault, and our fear will cloud our judgement, cut us off from love.

Our task, as a religious and spiritual community, is to build and rebuild those connections, those bridges, those bonds between and among us. To affirm and reaffirm our human ideals and aspirations, our human potential to choose the good, to choose to live with love.

Through hundreds of years, the warning has been sounded:

Remember human that thou art dust and into dust thou shalt return.

Let those words be not a warning but a celebration of our human nature and our human potential, a celebration of our creation from the dust of eternity, stardust, earth dust, linking us together and linking all of us to all of life.

HEART TO HEART

When I wrote for the Newsletter what this sermon would be about I said the title was "Heart to Heart." I went on to write: Lately I've had to pay a lot of attention to the physiological functioning of my heart. There's been much conversation about my heart. Today I want to share with you what is IN my heart. I want to begin by reading two of my favorite poems.

E. E. Cummings

i thank You God for most this amazing
day:for the leaping greenly spirits of trees
and a blue true dream of sky;and for everything
which is natural which is infinite which is yes

(i who have died am alive again today,
and this is the sun's birthday;this is the birth
day of life and love and wings:and the gay
great happening illimitably earth)

how should tasting touching hearing seeing
breathing any—lifted from the no
of all nothing—human merely being
doubt unimaginable You?

(now the ears of my ears awake and
now the eyes of my eyes are opened)

PRAISE FOR WHAT RISES
By Holly Elaine Horn

I offer praise...for what rises:
sun and moon and stars—
the awakening each morning of the body, thick with dreams.

Let us praise children who fall down
and pick themselves up in skinned redness;
children who rise, bruised, with tears and courage.

Praise for the holy tropism of plants, wise and blindly
reaching up through soil—
praise for the bread which puffs and bubbles in the oven,
praise for the bread which rises.

Let us praise the earth's currents rising, mystical
from its molten core.
Let us praise the spirit of people
crushed by oppression—
across the generations rising up.

Praise for the solemn flight of birds,
Praise for what rises...
Praise: for raising our voices.
For raising our children:
Praise for raising a garden, a roof;
for raising our hands in greeting, in blessing,
in protest.

Let us offer praise for what rises:
the sap of maples;
the passion of wise and blindly mingling souls and bodies;
springtime rises this way in the blood, like a tide-line
to the flush of the skin.
Praise be—
Praise be—

Praise for what rises within us, sure and true.
for what rises among us, eternal, new.

Let us offer praise for what rises,
joyful and glorious on this day:
the ancient promise renewed,
the beginning again and again in love.

Praise ...for what rises.

In describing the human condition, it is often said that we humans are the only creatures who know we will die. That is a great truth and indeed that knowledge does shape our lives. It is always there with us- but usually we relegate it to the very edge of our consciousness where we can ignore it as much as possible. We nod wisely when we read these words or hear them in a sermon, but we don't often go any deeper. We don't spend much time thinking about our own death unless we have to. Facing our mortality is not, for most of us, some- thing we do by any choice. But sometimes, sometimes we must. Prob- ably many of us have had occasion to do so. Probably most of us have had some sort of experience that has whispered to us, or maybe even shouted, "You are going to die. And it may be sooner rather than later." Some of you have shared your experiences with me. You've told me what's happened and how it's affected you how it's changed you. For I think we all agree that facing our mortality is a transforming experience.

Not long ago, in a sermon about spiritual crises, I told you about how, when I was in my 20s, with three young children, I was told by my doctor that I had deep seated and serious cancer. As it turned out, I did not have cancer, but for the two weeks between the two diag- noses, I had to face the shaking possibility that I, a young mother of three children who NEEDED me, might die.

When the second doctor assured me that I didn't have cancer, I felt more than relief. I felt a most profound sense of gratitude and ever since, not a day has gone by that I have not felt that gratitude, that thankfulness for my life. The intensity of my response has waxed and waned over the years, but it has never been lost. And I was happy to keep that state indefinitely, happy to be a person who was alive, healthy and grateful. I had faced my mortality, tested my theology and found it served well.

Fast forward to January, 1996. After months of medical tests and agonizing decisions, our daughter Martha had spinal cord surgery, with very upsetting results. In the midst of all this stress, I began hav- ing chest pains. Finally, after a really severe attack at 11 p.m., alone in the Port Authority, I called my doctor. After several tests, my cardiologist told me I had coronary artery disease, that my pain was angina, and after tests to discover where my arteries were blocked, I would either need angioplasty or bypass surgery. This also meant that I was a prime candidate for a heart attack. This was serious business.

Most of you already know this story. And you know that the tests finally showed no blockage, and that medicine seems to be controlling the angina and that I am in no danger. You know all this because I told you. And also because you could see that sometimes I was in pain and having a hard time. And you have seen my relief, my joy at the good news. Relief, joy, gratitude, yes. And that keen, huge, nearly over-whelming appreciation of life at an even greater intensity that I felt that first time as a young mother.

Then all I could think about was my children, and how they need-ed me, how I could not possibly leave them. This time it's different. Well, of course I've grown and changed a lot in 30 years, experien-tially, theologically, spiritually. I was sustained then by my faith, hope and love. Those are what sustain me now. But the context is different, my children are grown, but I still don't want to leave them. And Wally, too, of course. All those bonds are just as strong. But now I also am living in the grip of a powerful call to ministry. And how could I possibly leave it? The vision of this congregation, what it is, what it could become, the bonds I feel with you, each member and friend. How could I possibly leave?

For I believe we have a mission together. And it is a supremely important mission. It is, quite simply, to save the world. We are here, together, building this religious/spiritual community so that we can save the world, one person at a time. We are her to discover and artic-ulate and share and proclaim the good news: That faith and hope and love are not the property of any one religion or sect or denomination or political party, are not bound up in rules or dogma, but are avail-able to every person, every living soul, each unique and precious per-son. We have a shared vision, shared among us, and a vision to be shared as widely as possible. We have principles and purposes which people, children and adults, can really live by.

And we are beginning to learn about and build true community, in which we care for and about one another. This is hard to do. We have learned to be separate, to take care of ourselves, not to ask much and not to give much, especially if we don't know one another extremely well.

We are hurried and we are harried. We guard our time and our emotions. Most of us have not had or do not have the experience or tradition of caring for one another. We don't bring food when people are sick or in trouble. We don't offer transportation. We don't send cards of flowers or make calls. We feel awkward, afraid we might intrude or be rejected or inappropriate. It's easier and safer just to show up on Sunday and sing a hymn about love and caring. Maybe this is what is best. Maybe this is all everyone really truly wants.

All I know is this: When things were toughest and I was rushing between home and hospital and I was worried and scared, I needed every kind word, every hug that any of you gave to me. And I remember all those years ago when I was sick and people brought food and sat with me and listened to my fears and worries and didn't try to fix it, just listened and sometimes held my hand. And I think, I really do, that times haven't changed that much and that is what people need to receive and need to give today. Tell me if I'm wrong.

Last but far from least, I think everyone needs a community with whom they can celebrate, share the joy of living, share the milestones of life, both the sorrows and the happiness. Share pain, grief, loss. Share the wonder, the appreciation of living. Share the feelings and experiences that make us want to sing! Share when our senses are awake, and our reason, our compassion, our conscience, our vision. Share when we want and need to praise what rises, when we want to give and strengthen our faith, our hope and our love.

We need a community where we can stretch forth our hands, not hoping but trusting, knowing that others will be reaching too. A community of faith, hope and love where we will meet heart to heart.

THE NAMES OF GOD

In his poem about six blind men experiencing an elephant for the first time, John Godfrey Saxe writes how each man had a different opinion as to what an elephant is: a wall, a spear, a snake, a tree, a fan, a rope! Yet all were in the wrong! Our experience, and therefore our perceptions, can never be completely isolated or completely free of influences and associations. The blind men were each able to experience, to know, only the part of the elephant that they could touch. They couldn't see the whole picture. Those of us human beings who have eyesight can know what an elephant looks like. But like the blind men, we can still only see part of the picture. We can't see the huge scheme, the infinity in which we, exist. How did everything and everything, really begin, and why? Throughout human history the most persistent and widespread response to these questions has been some sort of concept, of God.

God. People have struggled with and stretched and shaped the idea and meaning of God since the first glimmers of human awareness emerged. In earlier cultures, and in some today there were many Gods, or many manifestations of God. There were Gods of nature, Gods of fire, water, trees, animals, rocks. There was the Earth Mother. There was a whole cast of Gods who embodied human traits, both positive and negative. It's now thought that the very earliest Gods were in fact Goddesses, images of that which was of prime importance to those ancient ancestors of ours, fertility. The reproductive ability of people, of animals and plants, of the earth, really. The fertility, the reproductive power, yes, of the earth itself.

But at some point, probably over a long transition period, the dominant God became a male God. Now there are still female Gods and animal Gods in some cultures, but religions based on a patriarchal, very definitely male God are, Judaism, Christianity and Islam. These religions dominate large segments of the world's population. Buddhism, another of the world's largest religions, also developed with a central, male image, the Buddha. And Confucius, the great teacher of China, was also male. And Hinduism, though it has many

Gods and a variety of images, has as its center, the one God, Brahma, who is traditionally characterized as a male. The Gods of Africa, too, seemed to be dominated by male images.

Now the Judeo Christian Gods of Western culture taught that God was a supernatural, personal, judging, male being with whom people could communicate (some people more than others) and who cold intervene in the laws of the universe and in people's personal lives.

The Hebrew's God was a covenantal God. There was a mutual agreement between the people and their God. Their God was a stern, judgmental patriarch and a protector, male, and yet far, far above all humans. But though this God was not to be portrayed by any image, "no graven image," still, the words of the Bible, the verbal imagery, seem to point to a very masculine entity with very human characteristics.

With the development of Christianity came Jesus, as intermediary, as intercessor with God. Jesus was the human incarnation of God, human, so easier to relate to. Instead of the Law, as the Jews had, the Christians had Jesus as a role model. That's what he was at first, a spirit-filled, God-filled human figure. But later the church decreed that he was God (another addition to the male view of God) and the doctrine of the Trinity was born.

Then, during the enlightenment, the Age of Reason, the idea of Deism developed: the concept of God as first cause; the great clock maker who created everything according to natural law, set it all in motion and needed to do nothing further. Reality was to be understood or interpreted through human reason rather than through divine revelation. And yet, and yet, even with the divine clock maker, almost an abstract term, even though interpreting this through reason, still, isn't strange that God remained a male figure in the language used to describe this abstract clock maker. But the theistic view had remained as well and has been the basis of the most naive and the most sophisticated theology. Conservative and fundamentalist preachers picture God as the all - powerful, loving, judging patriarch whose laws, written in the Bible, must be taken literally and obeyed.

But liberal Protestant theologian Paul Tillich called God "the ground of being"; for him, God is the structure of everything that exists, or as Alfred North Whitehead put it, "the principle of concretion." It is the glue that holds everything together. Unitarian theologian Henry Nelson Weiman thought of God as the principle of creativity functioning in all things. He spoke of God as creative interchange; the process by which we really listen to one another and arrive at new levels of spiritual awareness because we have made real contact with one another. Martin Buber, the great Jewish theologian, found God in what he called the I-thou relationship. Simply put, what Buber says is that there are 2 ways of relating to people. We can see them as objects or it which serve our needs. Or we can see them as subjects or thou who are unique human beings like ourselves. We relate to God as we relate to each other, as I-thou rather than I-it; as we care for another's well-being as we do our own.

I wish I had grown up hearing about and experiencing the theologies of Tillich, Weiman and Buber, but I didn't. What I heard when I was growing up , what I heard when I was little, was that God seemed like Santa Claus, or that Santa Claus seemed like God. He was a man, judging, looking down on me, watching to see if I would behave myself. Now I was taught that I had this soul, which was sort of like a white blob in my abdomen, and when I did anything wrong, it got a black spot on it. And God, up there, could look down and right through whatever I was wearing and see that soul and those black spots, and he didn't like black spots. So I thought that most of the time he didn't like me very much because most of the time I had a few. Now this God had a black book, which he wrote things down in. I didn't really relate to that God very much, except that he was spying on me.

I talk to people now that have grown up with a different kind of God, a friendly God, a God that they walk hand in hand with. A God that loves little children. That wasn't my experience, growing up in a rigid Catholic Diocese in Buffalo, New York. And that image stayed with me. Also, another part of my image of God was Jesus dying on the crucifix. If any of you grew up in a Catholic home, you probably had a crucifix with Jesus on it. Jesus was suffering, and bleeding, and he hung there over each person's bed. And that was scary. Not only was I judged, but it was very scary to see this suffering Jesus hanging over my bed. It was the first thing I saw when I went into my room, and the last thing I saw when I got into my bed.

Now also when I went to church, I was told that the priest was God's surrogate here on earth. There were no women priests, only men. And that was because only men were made in God's image. I think that some of us were taught that all of us were made in God's image. I was taught that men were made in God's image and that women were sort of just left over. So when I went to church, not only did I see a male God hanging on the crucifix, not only did I hear stories that he was watching me, but I was told those stories by a priest who was God's representative here on Earth, who also had the power to judge me when I went to confession and told my sins. Now all this was considered normal for a child my age, a Catholic child in Buffalo. I don't think anyone wondered what they were doing to my poor little psyche. It was considered a good religious training for the future. Of course the results are that I'm a Unitarian Universalist minister.

So, maybe it works! But it took me a long time to get there. A very long time. And I was a very angry person without even knowing it. It didn't occur to me that I could have said, "I don't like this image of God and I'm going to think up another one. No, I thought that the only one available was the one that I was taught. and because I didn't like it much I felt very guilty as well as angry. It was a hard way to grow up and a lot of hard lessons to learn, thinking about how to deal with this very important part of my life. Now I was sent to religious instructions, every Sunday and every Monday afternoon, released time, until I graduated from High School. And I got a hundred on my religion exams, I was very good. And I learned things like this: If a woman is on the top of a tall building, and is being chased by a rapist, and jumps off the building to escape being raped, is she committing the sin of suicide? No, she is not. She is jumping off the building to escape rape, not to kill herself. This the kind of thing I learned in Sunday School and religious instructions. But I never heard much about what I hear now. About God is love. About my relationship to God and never being judged. I never thought that anything like that was possible.

When I got married, I married someone who was in his second Catholic University, so obviously we were going to make a very good Catholic team. We went on our honeymoon and when we got back, the next morning was Sunday. When we woke up Wally said, "Oh, we better hurry or we'll be late for mass!" And I said, "What for?" I'll never forget that because I never thought I would say a thing like that in my life. I was never in touch, you might say, with my feelings about God. But after I said what for, the damn broke, and I really asked myself, what for. The upshot of it was that we didn't go to church very much for a number of years. Now finally, we found Unitarian Universalism, and we found it by reading ads in the newspaper. I hope that a lot of people are about to do that in the Englewood area. That's what happened with us. However it took us two years of reading the ads before we went to the Buffalo Unitarian Universalist Church, so that's why I thought we better start running them here pretty quick.

I got to Unitarian Universalism, and I heard a lot of interesting things. I felt like I was basically a very religious person, but I was not comfortable with the idea of God. A friend of mine couldn't understand how I could be religious and yet be agnostic. But I thought it was easy. It took me all these many years to finally get to the point where, I guess how I would describe it is, that at last I feel comfortable, with God. I can talk to others and not even need to qualify every statement. I can hear what others are saying., and not feel defensive, or not think that I had to ask them a lot of questions or argue with them. God is a word that I can choose to use, in order to communicate. Its a word I can choose to use in order to be in touch with other people, with myself, and with the potential that exists in us, and between us, and among us. And it seems to me that more and more people are choosing to be open to that "G" word. To thinking about and wanting to talk about their spiritual quest, their spiritual development, open to the possibilities of creative interchange with others and with themselves.

For many years God was a term too loaded with negative meaning and connotation. I just couldn't separate it from those painful, patriarchal, punishing images of my Catholic past. And I got along just fine without God, really. I was a religious person, as I said, an ethical person, growing spiritually, and I could do it all without using the "G" word. But as I continued on my religious journey and I came to terms with my religious past, as I began to seek and value human connectedness, something was happening. A new concept, a new understanding of God was struggling to birth in my consciousness, and it has been a wonderful, freeing experience.

And just as the blind men each had a piece of the puzzle, I think that we too each have a piece of that infinite definition of God. We can share those definitions, we can enlarge our understanding of each other, and therefore with God. We don't have to agree, and we don't have to convince each other, and we don't have to win.

I've had many conversations with many Unitarian Universalists as I struggle to not only to understand what I mean, but what they mean when they use the word "God." When someone says, I don't believe in God, I ask what they mean by God. If they say something like, well I don't believe in a transcendent being that orders and arranges my life, I can say that I agree with them. I, too, do not envision God as a fatherly figure in the sky who controls what happens here on earth. I don't imagine God that way , and some other people don't imagine God that way, but you may, and we can still both be Unitarian Universalists, which is one of the great strengths of our denomination.

If someone says that they imagine the divine as the figure of a nurturing mother, maybe they call it Goddess, I understand that understanding, though its not mine. I don't imagine God to be either male or female. Yet, we can both be Unitarian Universalists. Some people don't like the word God at all. It had bad connotations for them, just as it did with me. They feel uncomfortable with it. I can understand that, but since we are both Unitarian Universalists, I can also expect my language and my understanding will be respected, even if you don't agree with me.

I chose to use the word God because it has developed a deep resonance for me. Its a word with many dimensions. A word with enormous power to symbolize the unnameable, something more, which I experience in my daily life. Now this symbol, as I said, doesn't point towards an anthropomorphic figure. And this symbol does not stand for a hierarchical arrangement. This symbol, God, for me, points towards a process, the process of all creation, in space and in time. Now I'm a part of this process, so are you, so is my cat. And the bowl off fruit on my table, and the tree outside my window. And the stars that I cannot see, hurtling through space beyond. All that is part of the process that I call, God.

My life is a living cell in this larger body called life, which I cannot understand, and which I absolutely believe to be whole, and to be holy. Because I like the word God, that's what I call this process, which includes all life and all depth, and the spaces in between. You may not agree with me. Your views may be very different than mine. Because we are Unitarian Universalists we can talk about our different understandings. We can respect each others language. We can try to listen to one another, as we talk about what we believe. Images have great power in our lives, individually and collectively. According to anthropologist Clifford Gerz, religious symbols shape our cultural ethos, and define the deepest values of the society and the persons in that society. "Religion," Gerz writes, "is a system of symbols, which acts to produce powerful, pervasive and long lasting moods and motivations in the people of a given culture."

These symbols have psychological and political effects, because they create the deep seated attitudes and feelings that lead people to accept social and political systems that correspond with those symbols. Even people who say they don't believe in God or who don't participate in institutional religion, or who don't belong to or attend a church or synagogue, even people who have rejected religious symbolism on a conscious level, are still influence by it, because symbols can't just be rejected, says Gerz, they must be replaced. The symbol of God as a white male has been the basis for sexism and racism throughout our history.

Its amazing to realize how people have bought into that system, because the symbolism is so powerful, such a powerful given that it was not questioned, even by those who it repressed. Martin Luther King, Jr., was a religious leader in the struggle for civil rights. And he was so powerfully effective because he was able to give new meaning to religious symbols. Liberation theologians and feminist theologians do the same thing. And so do right wing fundamentalists.

Or rather I'd say they solidify old meanings and old symbols. Now this is why I believe it is important for us to pay attention to the religious symbolism in our lives. The language, the structures, the traditions. We need to explore their influence in our lives, and we need to find out ways of communicating with words and symbols that describe the values that we want to put forth in our lives and in our culture. God is certainly one of those symbols.

Many Unitarian Universalists, and I was one of them, have had the same experience that Shud had in *The Color Purple*. When I found out that I thought God was white and a man, I lost interest, she sighed. The first step is to find out what negative and outworn symbols may be influencing us. The next step is to decide what we're going to do about it. Then, even though we may reject those symbols, instead of losing interest, as Shud said she did, but really didn't, we must work to replace them, because we can't live in a spiritual vacuum. Let's celebrate the fact that we don't have to. We can choose new symbols, new meanings for our lives, while respecting the best of the old.

Whether or not we use the word God, whatever language we choose to convey our values, it is our choice. We are free to choose. We are responsible, we are creative, we are religious and spiritual human beings. Let us rejoice in that fact and not fear to use all of the potential that we have as religious beings. When we reach out to others with our joys and sorrows. When we share our dreams and our fears, when we offer comfort or challenge, when we embrace or support or lean on each other. When we offer words of wisdom, of hope, or forgiveness or encouragement, or humor or love. When we speak to each other with openness and honesty and trust, we are in the presence of the most ultimate, by whatever name we may call it. I seek it, I seek to share it and I celebrate it.

There's something else I'd like to share with you. A friend of mine sent me the words to a song in our hymnbook. It's #23, "Bring Many Names." I hope we'll be able to sing it together soon.

Bring many names, beautiful and good;
celebrate in parable and story,
holiness in glory, living loving God:
hail and hosanna, bring many names.

Strong mother God, working night and day,
planning all the wonders of creation,
setting each equation, genius at play:
hail and hosanna, strong mother God!

Warm father God, hugging every child,
feeling all the strains of human living,

caring and forgiving till we're reconciled:
hail and hosanna, warm father God!

Old, aching God, grey with endless care,
calmly piercing evil's new disguises,
glad of new surprises, wiser than despair:
hail and hosanna, old, aching God!

Young, growing God, eager still to know,
willing to be changed by what you've started,
quick to be delighted, singing as you go:
hail and hosanna, young, growing God!

Great, living God, never fully known,
joyful darkness far beyond our seeing,
closer yet than breathing, everlasting home:
hail and hosanna, great, living God!

BRING MANY NAMES
Words by Brian Wren
© 1989 Hope Publishing Co.,
Carol Stream, IL 60188
All rights reserved. Use by permission.

RELIGION AND PSYCHOLOGY

Religion and psychology, what's the difference? Is there a difference? Is today's religion a form of therapy as some have claimed? Well, first off, I must tell you that though I've had training as a pastoral counselor, with all of the group work that requires, and though I do pastoral counseling, I have never been, as they say, "in therapy." This is not to say that I've had a problem-free life, or that I have a bias against therapy or therapists. Quite the contrary. I was raised, educated and came of age in a time and a milieu which assumed a psychological cause for every problem and illness. Nurture won out over nature every time. And yet the fact remains, positively disposed as I was and am to therapy, I myself have never, you might say, benefited from it. However, as a child, as a young adult, a wife, a mother, a teacher, I've lived in a world in which psychology played a very important part, as it certainly does today. Children's development, at least then, was totally or nearly so the result of good or bad parenting. Autistic children were made that way by their mothers. Homosexuality was the result of overly involved mothers and cold, distant fathers. Pregnant women had morning sickness because they were rejecting motherhood. The only child was destined for a life of trouble. And there was more. Men had heart attacks because they had Type A personalities. People got ulcers because they worried too much. When you hated your job or your life you were maladjusted. If you were a solitary type you needed to be socialized.

But there was one area in which psychology had no role at all — it was never mentioned, it was never invoked — and that was the religion in which I was raised: Roman Catholicism. The question that we Unitarian Universalists often ask today — in what language do we tell our religious story? — had a simple answer then. The language of the religious story was found in the law and the rules and the dogma of the church, and in the sacred scriptures as interpreted by priestly authority. If you disobeyed the rules, you were wrong. You didn't need help or insight or understanding, you needed penance. And a warning that if you didn't shape up you were going to hell. Guilt? Good. You're a sinner and you deserve it.

Psychology was basically the enemy of religion. At best, it was irrelevant. And that's still true in many conservative or fundamentalist religions today, although I do think that there's been one major change for the many who have turned to evangelizing through marketing skills and politics, both of which are based on psychological research. However, though psychology may inform the method, it has little or nothing to do with the message.

For Unitarian Universalists, though, it's quite different. Our language, our story, our message is framed by psychology. I have never experienced Unitarian Universalism outside that framework. Our first principle — respect for the worth and dignity of every person — our strong commitment to the authority of individual conscience, and now our growing awareness and respect for the interdependent web, these Unitarian Universalist basics reflect our commitment to the importance of insight and understanding of the human personality. I would doubt that there's a Unitarian Universalist today whose way of perceiving and thinking about human beings from the self to society hasn't been shaped and formed by psychology. And because of this, Unitarian Universalism, as a religion and as an institution, is inextricably bound up to psychology. And I accept this as a condition of life as a Unitarian Universalist in this culture. And as long as we are in this framework, developing insight and understanding, respect, compassion, connectedness, then it is a positive thing. However, I see several dangers here. We joke about Unitarian Universalists having such open minds that everything falls out. And I worry sometimes, that we come perilously close to having this happen to Unitarian Universalism itself, both corporately and yes, individually. I fear that we often use psychology, psychological jargon, psychobabble, psychological stereotypes, psychological small talk in place of our story rather than to tell our story. We toss around words like depressed, psychotic, paranoid, neurotic, co-dependent, dysfunctional, as if we are communicating.

Often, quite the opposite is true. We use these terms to excuse irresponsible, harmful or unworthy behavior in ourselves and others, and we can become analytical and diagnostic in our relationships and in our communications. When we think in terms of diagnosing people, the next logical step, the next logical response, is treating people, fixing people, objectifying people, handling people, controlling people. Do we see a person as someone in the process of creation, in the process of becoming? Or do we see that person as a case? Do we see that person in terms of his or her talents, gifts and skills, or do we see the person in terms of his or her problems and lacks and deficiencies?

We substitute psychology for religion. We are more comfortable with psychological language than we are with theological language. It can be easier to label our self or others with a psychological disorder than it is to relate, to speak of what is really going on between us. It can be easier to speak to a therapist than to each other. Easier to trust a therapist than each other. Easier to accept a diagnosis, rather than to accept one another. Easier to use prescription medication, rather than feel. Easier to focus on feeling good than feeling real. Feeling real, that's harder, much harder.

And so it seems that often we don't deal adequately or realistically with pain or with suffering. We look to medicine for a fix. We look to psychology for a fix, too. A diagnosis, a therapy, a cure. Suffering is a negative to be done away with as quickly as possible. There is little respect or tolerance for suffering as a human condition, suffering for a purpose, or an ideal larger than one's self.

Our religion is not about cures. It's about healing. Our religion is not about therapy. It's about transformation. Transformation of the self and transformation of society. Psychology, too, is about change. One of the differences is that psychology focuses on the individual ego, and religion, in my view, has the larger goal of transforming society. That the world may become more loving, and more just. Psychology is about individual happiness, and well-being, and fulfillment. Religion — religion's about that, too.

Our Unitarian Universalism is still about those three so often cited basics: faith, hope and love. The need for faith, hope and love. The need for faith in a world of science and technology. The need for hope in a world now past the belief in human perfectibility or divine intervention. The need for love in a world that has trivialized and romanticized and eroticized the word and the response. A world in which love means "never having to say you're sorry."

And religion is about justice, too. As a Unitarian Universalist, I believe that there is no real religion that is not about justice. The challenge that we face is what I think Unitarian Universalism is all about. Not to fix people, not to fool them or placate them, not to ignore them, or be passive or give up on them, but to be with each other. Be present to each other. In our time and in our culture, what we call psychology is part of this process. But religion is more. It's wider, it's deeper. Religion has to do with body, mind, and yes, religion has to do with soul. It has to do with insight, awareness, and yes, it has to do with mystery. It has to do with the unity of all these aspects. It has to do with healing that goes beyond therapy to the spark of holiness that lives within each person. That spark does not need to be analyzed or defined or shaped or judged. It is to be affirmed, respected and loved. However we do this — with words, images, movement, music, with awe, and with reverence — however we touch this — from our reaching towards the vastness of the universe to the clasping of your hand in mine — our story is not just told, it is not just analyzed, it is not just quantified, it is lived and it is shared.

I want to tell you a story. It's a true story and it's a very Unitarian Universalist story. A few years ago, I attended a Unitarian Universalist leadership school. A summer program in July in the country, up north in Canada. Each day we were assigned a topic and we wrote in our journals, and then we shared copies of what we had written with others in our small group. Now one of the members in our group was a man named Art. He was about sixty. He was large, shy, and very ill at ease. And as he told his story, we began to understand. Art came from a Unitarian Universalist family. His father was a doctor, his mother was a teacher. Two of his brothers were also doctors, one was a lawyer, his sister was a writer.

Art was dyslexic. Of course, when he was a kid, no one knew about dyslexia. Art was just 'slow.' He was a poor reader, he was a 'dumb kid', he couldn't keep up. His family loved him, but it was tough being a non-reader in a family for whom reading was a central part of their lives together. When Art grew up he became a mechanic—a good one, he could fix anything. And he became a gardener, I think he could grow just about anything. He was active in his Unitarian Universalist church, but he remained very self-conscious and with a feeling that he was less, because he was slow, he was still that 'dumb kid', he was a poor reader.

Then, when he was sixty years old, his church, thinking they were doing a great thing, sent him to leadership school, where, surprise, he had to write every day and he had to show people what he had written. He slaved over every page. And things were okay until the fourth day. On that day the topic was transformation and transcendence. And when we shared our papers, Art realized that he spelled transcendence with an 'a' instead of an 'e' and it bothered him so much. "I'm so dumb," he said, "It's bad enough I can't spell," he said, "but I couldn't even copy the word right." We assured him that we didn't know the difference, but it made a difference to Art. He still seemed crushed.

The next day our group went for a walk through the woods and out into the sunlight of a beautiful flowering meadow. The sun was shining, the sky was blue, the butterflies hovered, and suddenly Liz, one of the women in our group, lifted her arms and began to dance. She ran and she swirled through the meadow shouting, "Transcen-DANCE! Transcen-DANCE! Art, you were right! It's transcen-DANCE! Thank you, Art!" And pretty soon all of us were leaping around in the meadow, right there with the butterflies, shouting, "Transcen-dance, Art! It's transcen-dance!" Art began to sway too, with his arms out. We looked at him. He stood there swaying, with the most amazing smile on his face. And then he reached out his hands and we all clasped hands in a circle there, moving back and forth. There in that circle stood Art, with that beautiful smile on his face. "Yes," he said, "Yes." Recently I read in his church newsletter that Art had died. I lift up this story in thanks for the gift of grace that we all shared that day in a summer meadow. It was the day that we got religion. It was the day that we shared the gift of "Yes." May we in this congregation share such gifts also.

EASTER: A SEASON OF RENEWAL

L ong before there was a Jewish religion or a Christian religion, before there was Passover or Easter, long before any religions as we know them existed at all, long before history or scripture were written down and put into books, men and women greeted the coming of spring with joyful celebration. Winter was frightening then. Each day the sun gave less light and stayed in the sky for a shorter period of time, and they wondered, what if it faded away entirely? What if it slipped down behind a mountain or into the sea and was too weak ever to rise again? In many cases the waning of the sun brought cold—sometimes extreme cold. Vegetation seemed to die. Birds and animals seemed to disappear. And the waning sun made the possibility of death frightening real. Yet each year the sun did return. It did become stronger once more. And with the sun vegetation also returned with the promise of flowers and fruits. Of renewed food supply that meant that life would continue. In their joy, people celebrated and held spring festivals to honor the sun and its great power to bring new life to all growing things.

Spring was also a time to celebrate fertility which was vital to keeping the clan, indeed the species, going. In neolithic and paleolithic times fertility was the chief subject of art and religion, as people sought to influence and ensure the continuity of people, of plants, of animals and of the earth itself. The oldest religious objects we have ever found are fertility figures of the mother goddess. Later, as people turned from hunting and gathering to agriculture, the mother goddess became the earth goddess and later became the mother of the dying god who -as vegetation -is born anew each spring. The god who died and rose again symbolizing the agricultural cycle, became a widespread religious concept. The death and the resurrection theme is certainly not exclusive to one religion or one culture.

Even the egg and the bunny rabbit, symbols that today are associated with the Christian festival of Easter and the secular festival of Easter, are much older than Christianity and were known in ancient times as symbols of fertility. The rabbit, or more technically the hare, was a symbol for the womb, and according to legend the hare, which is born with its eyes open, never blinked, never closed its eyes—and so seemed to symbolize ongoing life. Its Egyptian name is UN, meaning open. Like the moon, the hare was nocturnal and had a reproductive cycle of about a month. And it was also, as we know today, very prolific. The egg seemed almost a universal symbol and as such is very, very old and very profound. An ancient proverb says all life comes from an egg. The people of Polynesia, ancient India, Indonesia, Iran, Greece, Phoenicia, Latvia, Estonia, Finland, Central America, the west coast of South America, all had myths of a cosmic egg, an egg which gave birth to the whole universe.

In Indian mythology, the creator of all living things, came forth from a great golden egg which was formed in the primal waters, and one of the Hindu scriptures says, "In the beginning, this world was merely non-being. It was existent. It developed. It turned into an egg. It laid for a period of a year. It was split asunder. One of the two eggshell parts became silver, and one gold. That which was of silver is the earth. That which was of gold is the sky. What was the outer membrane is the mist. What were the veins are the rivers. What was the fluid within is the ocean. Now, what was born therefrom is yonder sun."

For the Samoans, the heavenly one, once lived in an egg which he broke into pieces and created the earth. And in the Greek myth, the silver world-producing egg was laid by the night and fertilized by the wind. The imagery is wonderful. And in Egyptian mythology, Geb, the earth, and Nut, the sky, together produced the egg from which came the universe. Eggs were said to be dyed and eaten in ancient Egypt, Persia, Greece and Rome. The Persians gave eggs as gifts at the vernal equinox. Both the hare and the egg were symbols of the spring goddess of fertility, Eastre, for whom Easter received its name.

So we see that spring, the coming of the sun, the renewal of the cycle of fertility, has been honored and celebrated throughout human history. Because of the deep power of those rites as an integral part of the human psyche, they were incorporated into Judaism and then into Christianity. And even now in our time, when many of us don't think very much about agriculture except as a hobby, and when fertility is an issue of control as much as it is of encouragement, even now when science has explained the cycles of the seasons and the nightly weather forecast is sometimes if not always right, even now we people at the end of the twentieth century respond even as those ancients did to the coming of spring. For us, as for them, it is a symbol of hope, of rebirth and of renewal. Of course Judaism and Christianity each have their particular faith's stories, as all religions do. For Jews, Passover marks the beginning out from oppression and becoming a people covenanted with God. For Christians, Easter tells the story of resurrection with its wide range of interpretations from literal to metaphoric. A story about sharing in the kingdom of God. Both faith's stories are stories of hope—hope for a better time to come.

Now I would guess that few if any of us here today take any of these stories literally. But we can take the universal human need, the ability or the will to hope, very seriously. It is perhaps our strongest link to all of humanity throughout history. Through hope, we are a part of something larger than ourselves. Through hope, we make the commitment to try to do the best we can. To love and to care and to nurture the best we can. To live our ideals by the best ideals we can. To live knowing that we are worthy of the gift of life. This commitment to hope gives ultimate meaning to life and therefore to death. Cycles of birth and death exist in nature on all levels. From the universe, to our galaxy, to our planet earth, our seasons, our individual lives, our body, our mind, even our feelings. All these move through cycles of generation and regeneration, rebirth and renewal. We are part of a cycle on every level, from the most basic to the most ephemeral. The universe is too vast, too far away, just too big for us to really comprehend. We can question, we can wonder, but we can't really know. And some human cycles are too close for us to understand—the working of the cells, the working of all those amazing parts of the body. Again, we question, we wonder, but we never will really know everything about them. The universe is working, our cells are working, but our knowledge is basically theoretical. The seasons of the earth are just about the right size, the right distance, for us to comprehend. We can see and we can experience and we can measure them.

So the seasons have become symbols for us of all of the other life cycles that we sense and wonder about. And so, we celebrate spring— season of hope, birth, renewal of life, as a metaphor for our own life and for all life. Between birth and death we experience many lesser births and deaths of the body, the mind, emotions and the spirit. Old ideas and relationships and habits die, sometimes peacefully, often painfully. We know suffering and we know grief. We reach into ourselves and we reach out to others for the solace and the nurture and the inspiration that we need. And gradually, gradually hope grows. We experience rebirth. In celebrating this Easter season, and all seasons, we acknowledge that possibility of rebirth and renewal that exists for each of us and all of us. We can learn, we can grow, we can reach out to others, we can effect change. We will know sorrow, joy, fulfillment, challenge, and maybe even a little boredom in between— but not much, not really. Because in the quiet times we can reflect and remember and appreciate and wait. We can live with faith. The faith that life is indeed worth living. The faith in ourselves, in others, that grounds and centers our lives. We can live with hope, hope that our efforts will bear good fruit. Hope for the future of our world. And we can live with love—intimate love for our families, our friends and ourselves, compassionate love for humanity, for all living things, for the interdependent web of all existence of which we are a part.

There is no formula that guarantees spiritual renewal. But there are many ways and many paths and many disciplines. Renewal can come when we open ourselves to the beauty and the power of nature—of life in all its myriad forms. Renewal can come when we allow ourselves to know and be known by other people. Renewal can come as we experience art, music, drama, poetry, dance. Renewal can come in times of suffering or grief, when we reach out and clasp hands. And renewal can come in our moments of silence. And our moments of laughter. Our moments of play, our moments of peaks, of valleys, and yes, in dailyness. All of these things will happen for us at many times in many places.

Sometimes new ideas and relationships are born, and sometimes the old ones are transformed and renewed. Throughout our lives and the life of the world, these cycles will continue. We all have our hopeful springs and our summers of growth, our nostalgic autumns, our winters of despair— each in its time, and each will pass. So when spring comes to us let's be sure to pay attention. Let's be sure to respond and to celebrate. Let's celebrate not only the growth that the season brings, but also the nurturing that we can receive and that we can give. Let's celebrate our common history, our potential to hope and to work for the good. Our human capacity to dream and hope that the bleakest times will be followed by sunlight, that cold will be followed by warmth, and that all of us, whatever our stories of faith, can share the story of human and universal hope. Throughout our lives and the life of the world, we hope.

MAKE A DIFFERENCE

There is nothing worse than indifference: indifference to God or humans, to life, to suffering or to unhappiness. If I were to give you one word that encompasses all the evils in life, it would be "indifference."

Elie Wiesel

Just as inertia produces despair — a despair so often so deep that it doesn't even know itself as despair - arousal and action would give us access to hope, and life would start to mend: not just life in its entirety but daily life, every individual life.

from *The Fate of the Earth* by Jonathan Schell

Sermon:

Then Abraham drew near and said, "Wilt thou indeed destroy the righteous with the wicked? Suppose there are fifty righteous within the city; wilt thou then destroy the place and not spare it for the fifty righteous who are in it?" And the Lord said, "If I find at Sodom fifty righteous people in the city, I will spare the whole place for their sake."

Abraham answered, "Suppose five of the fifty are lacking? Wilt thou destroy the whole city for lack of five? And He said, "I will not destroy it if I find forty-five there."

Again he spoke to Him and said, "Suppose forty are found there?" He answered, "For the sake of forty I will not do it."

Then he said, "Oh let not the Lord be angry, and I will speak. Suppose thirty are found there." He answered, "I will not do it if I find thirty there."

He said, "Suppose twenty are found there. He answered, "For the sake of twenty, I will not destroy it."

Then he said, "Oh let not the Lord be angry, and I will speak again but this once. Suppose ten are found there." He answered, "For the sake of ten I will not destroy it."

And the Lord went His way when He had finished speaking

to Abraham, and Abraham returned to his place.

Genesis 18: 23-33

When God wanted to destroy the city of Sodom because it was evil and corrupt, Abraham bargained with God that if there were even ten righteous people in the city, it would be spared.

Think of it. If there had just been ten righteous people, the city would have been saved. The people of Sodom probably weren't all BAD people. They probably weren't all WICKED people. Some were, but what about the rest? This was a big city. If there weren't ten righteous people, what were there?

There were passive, uncommitted, frustrated, turned off, burned out, indifferent, self-centered people. They'd given up hope that things could change. They'd insulated their feelings. They DIDN'T CARE or COULDN'T CARE or WOULDN'T CARE. They'd learned to narrow their focus to just their stomachs or their faces or their backs. Because to do otherwise might HURT them. It might INCONVENIENCE them. It might CHANGE them.

And the fact is, for us as well as for the people of Sodom, if we do nothing, if we don't care, if we don't actively work for the common good, if we're not part of the solution, then we're part of the problem. And our city, the city of the world, like the city of Sodom, is in danger of being destroyed.

What's the solution? We have to be righteous. Not BE right. DO RIGHT. And when we do RIGHT, then we make a difference.

Righteous, I never liked that word. I don't know how you feel about it, but to me the word righteous has always been a turn off. Righteous meant RIGHT. I'm RIGHT, so you must be wrong, unless you agree with me, of course. Righteous. The person who had all the answers. The person who was better than anyone else. Superior. Holier-than-thou. RIGHTEOUS. I NEVER liked that word.

Then I began my studies at New York Theological Seminary. And in my Hebrew Bible and New Testament courses, there was that word, righteous. And now my defining of that word has changed. I realized that I had equated being righteous with being self-righteous. And there is a big difference. Abraham and his people believed that God had given them a standard by which to live. They called that standard Law. Abraham was righteous because he had tried to live by that Law; to live according to his best; be in harmony with his God and his highest values.

We may call the standard by which we live, conscience. And our ideas about God may be very different from those of Abraham. In any case, our standard is based on what we know to be right and just, not for ourselves alone, but for ourselves as part of all humanity.

Righteous, trying to understand what the standard for our lives must be, then trying to live accordingly. Not living UP to something, but living BY it. We know that we fall short of standards of ultimate perfection. We're human beings. Righteousness isn't a goal, it's a process. Every day we commit ourselves to the process of working to bring our values and our actions into harmony; to become whole persons; people whose lives can make a difference. It isn't something we can do once and then forget about. It's a process we work at all of our lives.

In our Religious Values Seminars at the Unitarian Fellowship in Mt. Kisco, we discuss our ethical principles; the values we live by; our standards of conscience. Again and again, people have discovered that they agree on one very simple answer: Do unto others as you would have them do unto you. The Golden Rule. In varying forms, it's found in nearly every religion and culture in the world. It doesn't say do unto others who are just like you; your family or your friends or your church or your political party or your country; it says do unto others, all others, all of humanity. And it says DO. Not just think about it, DO.

We may not always have followed this rule. We've had wars, inquisitions, holocausts, terrorism, people shivering and starving in the streets. But we know these things are WRONG, because they violate human life, human dignity and human conscience. That's what makes us human; we are aware of the consequences of our actions. We know that to be human is to be responsible. We know that what we do affects others.

And what we DON'T do affects others too. When we read not to long ago about Imelda Marcos having two thousand pairs of shoes while some people in their country didn't have enough to eat, we knew it was WRONG. Then we look at our own lives. How many pairs of shoes do WE have? How much or our time, our energy, our money, should we use for others? What others? How much of a difference can we make?.

The world's problems are great. HUGE. We're just people. Small. What can we do? Whenever we start thinking or talking about all the things that need doing or fixing in our world, it's overwhelming. How can we act to make a difference? What should we do?

SHOULD. That's another word I never liked and I don't like it any better today. It's got more than four letters, but it's a BAD WORD. The S word. Let's not say the S word. Let's not ask what we SHOULD do. Let's ask what we CAN do; what we WILL do.

We can't save the whole world today, or this year, or even in our lifetime. But we can do our part. It's as if life is a huge mosaic. And each of us has tiny pieces, tesserae. Our task is to fit our little pieces into the design. Because without our pieces the design can't work, it has holes. And other pieces have nothing to connect to.

I believe this. I believe that what I do is important, that what I do is necessary. That, yes, the world depends on me. The world depends on each of us. Individually and collectively we do make a difference! We are making a difference.

Unitarians William Ellery Channing and Theodore Parker spoke out strongly for the abolition of slavery. Abraham Lincoln is remembered as the President who led our nation in ending slavery. Slavery ended because so many people were willing to stand firm and say "no more."

Susan B. Anthony and Elizabeth Cady Stanton worked tirelessly for women's rights, for suffrage. Women finally won the right to vote because so many people said yes.

Martin Luther King Jr. led the fight for civil rights. Civil rights were granted because of all the people who marched, who stood up for freedom and justice.

Adolph Hitler and the Nazis were responsible for the Holocaust in which millions of Jews were tortured and killed. The many, many people who looked away were also responsible. But some did not look away. They banded together and were responsible for smuggling many Jews to freedom. Their symbol was the flaming chalice, which has become our Unitarian Universalist symbol, a symbol of our commitment to action, to making a difference.

What can I do? I can affirm that by being a caring, concerned, loving person I am doing something positive and contagious. I can speak our for what I believe to be right. I can witness for peace and justice and human worth.

What will I do? I won't let the world's problems overwhelm me. I will choose one thing, however small and insignificant it may seem; one thing that affirms my values and beliefs, and I will act. I will DO that one small, insignificant thing. And then there'll be another thing to do and I'll do that. Maybe I can't be a congressperson; I can only write letters. I'll write. Maybe I'm not a national figure; I can speak from my pulpit, or my town hall, or my street corner. I'll speak. Maybe I can't give up all my goods; give all I have to the poor. But I can give. I will give actively. And I will do more than just feel sad and helpless and hopeless.

I will act more strongly, more positively than just shaking my head or wringing my hands.

I will believe that my life and my actions can encourage others to hope and act for the common good and because I believe this, my commitment and my ability to act will strengthen and grow.

I WILL DO WHAT I CAN and I will believe that my actions will make a difference. I will believe that my actions can encourage others to hope and act for the common good and because I believe this, my commitment and my ability to act will strengthen and grow.

Abraham tried to save the city of Sodom. He felt responsible. He cared that innocent people would suffer. We are part of the city of the world and we know that it is in danger; that not only are anger, greed and violence threatening the whole world but that passivity, indifference and despair may, in the last analysis, be the real forces of our destruction.

Abraham was part of a long, long human story. Will the story continue? Will our city be saved? Are there enough righteous people? Are you one of them? Am I? Believe it. We can make a difference. Each of us can make a difference.

I look around this room and I see people who are making a difference. People who teach our children. People who do the work of the church. Of the community. The care givers. The nurturers. The kind, thoughtful, helping hands. People who attend town meetings, school board meetings, who speak out on the issues, who stand up for peace and justice and human rights. I look around this room and I see people who are acting on what they believe to be right.

Are we passive? Sometimes. Are we frustrated? Sometimes. Are we turned off? Burned out? Sometimes. Are we uncommitted? No. Are we indifferent? No. Do we care? Yes. And sometimes it hurts. And sometimes it inconveniences us. And sometimes, sometimes it's changed us. Because that's what happens when we care.

Abraham left the city of Sodom before it was destroyed. But we can't leave the city of the world. This is where we must lead our lives. And we're going to live our lives FOR something. We're going to live our lives for GOOD. For JUSTICE. For PEACE. For LOVE. We're going to lead our lives for ALL of us. For we believe, we know, that we can make a difference.

I close with a prayer my mother has said every day of her life. And I know that she has made a difference.

O God of all People
We are thankful for our food
And remember the hungry.
We are thankful for health
We are thankful for friends
And remember the friendless.
We are thankful for freedom
And remember the oppressed.
May these remembrances stir us to service
And remember the sick.
That our gifts may be used for others.
Amen.

Meditation:

I invite you now to think of something that you are currently doing, now, this year, that makes a difference. Picture what it is that you do. Where are you? Who is involved? See the scene in your mind. What do you do? What happens? What good thing do you know happens as a result of what you do? Picture the good thing happening.

Now think of what else might happen, might begin or grow because of what you are doing. Cast your mind outward, see the effects of your action widening, widening. Moving outward like the ripples from one small stone dropped into a pool of water. Trace one of these ripples. What might it be? What might have happened, may yet happen for which your action was one thing, however small, that was needed? Just sit for a moment and see, feel in your imagination, those ripples in the water of life.

Now think of something you are going to do next. Something that you can and will do. One small thing. What will it be? Something in your family? Your Society. Your community? Something involving one other person, or many? One thing you will do, that will make a difference. How will it start? When? Picture that moment, the moment you begin. Do it. You can. We can each make a difference.

Benediction:
> Roots hold me close
> Wings set me free
> Spirit of life
> Come to me, come to me.
>
> My we dedicate ourselves to preserving and nurturing
> That spirit of life
> In all people, in all places, wherever it may be found.

May we go in peace knowing that we will make a difference.

I HAVE A DREAM

D r. Martin Luther King Jr. had a dream for all of humanity. It was a vision of possibility that inspired a nation. A dream of equality, liberty and justice for all. All races, all classes, all people. And his dream also included not only that day, but the process by which we might obtain it. The process, the principle, of non-violence. He never separated the parts of his dream. He never separated the journey from the destination. He lived with hope and faith in his dream, and also in the dreaming, in the process, the journey towards that dream. He lived with the belief, the confidence, the faith that non-violence was the way, the only way of life, the way to a life more abundant- the way to a good life for all people. The people who were inspired by Martin Luther King Jr.'s dream, who saw change through non-violence, were often met with terrible violence, but the dream lived. People who joined in peaceful witness, peaceful protest were reviled, or hurt, or killed. But the dream lived. Martin Luther King Jr. himself was gunned down and killed most violently.

But still the dream lived, and it lives today. Martin Luther King died without seeing the realization of his dream. He's often compared with Moses, a great leader with a great dream who made the journey to the promised land, but never arrived, never crossed over. The closest he got was to see the land of his dreams spread out before him, to look down from a mountain. But he died before he could enter. Martin Luther King Jr. understood that story. He understood that the important thing is the trying. Having the dream, and dedicating his life to the dream. Seeing the possibility, having faith, knowing that the dream will happen someday, was enough. I been to the mountain, he said, I've seen the promised land.

We all have dreams, each one of us . We have all sorts of dreams, some are very personal, some silly, some embarrassing, some really important with a larger scope. Dreams are different from goals. Goals may be part of our dreams, but dreams are more. To take a prosaic, personal and perhaps rather silly example, you might have the goal of losing weight, losing 20 pounds. You could write it down, like a resolution-LOSE 20 POUNDS! But the dream of losing 20 pounds, that's different. You dream of what it's like to lose 20 pounds, to be 20 pounds thinner. You dream of how you look, you dream of how it feels. You dream of what you do, of the good things that happen, of the compliments you receive. Without the dream, you're unlikely to reach your goal.

Do you remember your childhood dreams? Christmas, birthdays, adventures, dreams of being loved. Dreams of magic, of fantasy land. Dreams of simple things, a new toy, a pet, new shoes, a ring in a box of Crackerjacks. A friend, maybe a room of your own. And do you remember when you first became aware of the problems and the challenges of the larger world, of poverty, and suffering, and injustice? Do you remember when you first realized that you could make a difference? And do you remember when you became afraid that you couldn't make a difference? Have you made the journey from idealism, optimism, enthusiasm to discouragement and disillusionment, apathy? And have you gone on to a new level of commitment, to choosing your cause, to choosing your stand, your vision, and staying with it? Have you kept your dream and commitment to making your dream a reality?

Have you noticed that rarely, if ever, are you the only person in your dream? Dreams are meant to be shared. Both the dream itself and the process of realizing the dream. Ten years ago I began to dream of becoming a minister. But first, I tried to deny the dream. It wasn't possible. It was foolish. And my dream wouldn't go away. My dream was growing out of my relationships with others, as we worked together to build community. As the work and the relationships and the community grew, so did my dream of ministry grow. At last I shared my dream, tentatively at first, and very self-consciously. But people supported me. They affirmed my dream. And as I shared that dream, I began to believe that I could do it. I began to seek how I could do it.

And finally, I did it. And along the way, many people supported my dream, and celebrated with me, as it became a reality. Gradually then, my dream of ministry took on a clearer focus. I dreamed of a Unitarian Universalist congregation that would be truly open and accepting, that would welcome and celebrate diversity, and would find a way past racial and sexual, and hierarchical stereotyping, to form a community where black and white, straight and gay, old and young, rich and poor, all could be themselves and yet together more than themselves.

What a DREAM. And here I am. My dream of ministry is a dream of sharing- of equality, of challenge, and it's a dream of hard work. It's a dream of healing, and it's a dream of love. And I know that it's a dream of possibility. I know that I to may never reach the promised land. But I also know that the journey is worth whatever effort I'm able to make.

Four years ago, I preached a sermon on this very Sunday, about dreams, and I described my dreams for this new, very new society. I found that description in my files. Let me read it to you: Let me share with you my dream for this society. We gather for Sunday morning service. What a beautiful congregation. African American, Hispanic, Asian, White, Gay, Lesbian, straight, singles, partners, older, younger and from a variety of religious traditions. The children are with us for the first part of the service. We sing, we have a story, today, someone plays the drums as a prelude, and the children do some music too. Then they go off to religious education. The older children meet with their leaders. They have a time of sharing and getting better acquaint-ed. They may have a story and an activity. Today they are talking about peace making. The pre-schoolers have a similar schedule. They're at a cozy meeting spot and have fun making collages. The older children meet in the library. They too discuss peace making. How to handle conflict in their daily lives. They are planning a meet-ing with the children from a sister congregation here in town, and maybe they will go skating.

The adults have several joys and concerns to share, and the announcements and sharing time are lively. We have had a death in the congregation, and many people attended the funeral. They offer sympathy and support. A new baby is here for the first time. We ooh and ah. A couple announces their coming wedding, and we applaud. Another gay couple speak of how happy they are to have found a reli-gion that offers them a beautiful ceremony of holy union.

We are staffing the homeless shelter next week and plans are made. Our community choir is meeting weekly, and we'll sponsor a concert in April. A new adult education course is being planned. And a course on Unitarian Universalism begins soon. The monthly UU Bible study group is going strong and the parent's group will be meeting. We welcomed 3 new people into membership bringing our total to 97. We sing rousing songs and end with the quietly beautiful Spirit of Life. After the Social Hour, a group take off for a Gospel concert in the city. And several other groups head off to have lunch together. Teachers, RE Director and minister meet for a short evaluation and check in on how the programs are going. We store our things in the new storage area and get ready to leave. We'll see each other tomorrow at the Martin Luther King Jr. Birthday celebration.

This is still what I wrote then. My dream will take the efforts of many people, not just mine. My dream must be shared in order to become a reality. Sharing the dream means that we must find ways to share hopes, fears and feelings. To share not just a goal statement, but the story, the picture, the vision. We must share our ideas, plans and processes for journeying towards that dream. And then I wrote, if no one shares my dream, it will never become a reality. That happens sometimes. And if it does, I would hope that I could learn from the experience. I would hope that I would not become bitter. I would hope that I would not despair. I would hope that I would not give up. I would hope that I would find some aspects of my dream that could be shared. And that I would remember that trying is what matters.

It's fascinating to compare my 1990 dream, with our reality in 1994. Then we were just starting out. I had a dream and I had a hope that I would find people that would share that dream. Now my dream has become our dream. That's how I think of it now. Our dream. Our hopes. Our work. Our shared ministry. It wasn't a dream I could force on anyone. It wasn't a dream I could impose on any one. It was a dream I could speak of, and I dream I could offer. It was a dream I could act on. And you have brought your dreams and together we are building something new, weaving all of our dreams together. But I can't, we can't, know for sure how it will all turn out. It's going to be a long journey, I hope, building, falling, working, caring, believing,— believing that what we are doing is important, valuable, necessary, and having faith, we all need faith, and hope and love. We need faith in our dreams, faith that they're worthwhile dreams, just as we are worthwhile. We need hope, hope that tomorrow we'll be a little further on. Understand a little more. See and know just a little more. Share just a little more. We need love, love for ourselves, our neighbors, our journey, today, not because we've made it, not because we've succeeded. Love for the trying. Love for the living of it. Love for the struggle of it. Love for ourselves as vulnerable, fallible dreamers. Love for ourselves just as we are. Dreaming is important. Not success or failure, but dreaming, trying, hoping, loving, affirming. We may never get to the Promised Land, but we are living it into existence. The Promised Land exists only because of our vision of it. It exists only as we live it as much as we can, here and now. And we always know that there's more.

When Wally and I got married we were young and pretty ignorant, although we didn't think so then. Why did we marry? Because we had a dream, a vision of a shared life, a home, a family. A life that we could build together that would be more than we could do alone. We couldn't have predicted what that life has turned out to be. And our children, we couldn't have described what their lives would be like, who they'd be. We couldn't know it if we had many years or few. But we had glimpses. We had a dream, a picture, almost, but not quite beyond our grasp. Somehow, somehow, though faint, it was real. And we had faith in and hope and love for that dream and the journey, and somehow we recognized our dreams in the realities of today. That's how it is with dreams. We don't always know the particulars. We don't always have a precise blueprint. We may have many surprises. We may sometimes say, "Who could have ever predicted." And yet, looking back, we recognize that dream in our lives. It has shaped our lives, it had kept us open to the possibilities.

Dreams are made of tears as well as laughter. Pain as well as joy. Brick walls as well as doorways. Clouds and mists and fog and storms, as well as sunlight and clear sailing. The most important thing of all, yes!, the most important thing of all, is to believe, to have faith, and to know that it's worth it! We each have dreams, many dreams. And I hope we can share our personal dreams as well as the dreams for this society, this beloved community. May it be a place where we, the dreamers, can find and give inspiration, support and affirmation, for those ideas and dreams which give meaning and purpose to each and all of our lives.

Desmond Tutu wrote: We must remember that liberation is costly, and it needs unity.... We must hold hands, and refuse to be divided.... Let us be filled with hope. Let us be those who respect one another.

WHY?

I begin with two readings, both by unknown authors:

We know the mechanics of reproduction. Our young people are attending the human sexuality classes and they'll know even more than we do. We have computer dating to match people up. We have amniocentesis to find out about our babies before they are born. We have fortune tellers too, astrologists and palmists. We have biologists, psycho-biologists, micro-biologists...we have psychoanalysis and handwriting analysis, and weather forecasters and future forecasters, archeologists, and we're all asking what, how why? We want to solve the mystery, we want to learn the secret, we want to know!

Second reading:
Why did the world begin, and how?
I asked a dog, a pig, a cow.
Where are we going? How will it end?
I asked a fish, I asked a hen.
This is what they said to me.
I listened very carefully.

And now I'll pass it along to you,
Woof, Woof; Oink, Oink;
Cluck, cluck, Moo, Moo
And the fish said, (), ()

And that I think is how some people feel about all these questions that we keep constantly running into. Why? Why is the world the way it is? Why am I what I am? Why are you the way you are? Why do bad things happen? Why do good things happen? Why am I here? Why do I care? Why am I asking why? I don't know the answers to all those questions, but I'm pretty sure of one thing. Since earliest times people have asked why, have wondered, and speculated, had more questions, many more questions, than they've ever had answers.

And our degree of comfort with questions and our need for certainty of answers has determined and shaped our religions, our theologies, both individually and collectively.

Unitarian Universalists are questioners. We love questions. Probably most of us have been asking why since we were little children. We're such noted questioners that it's said that when Unitarian Universalists are being persecuted, their tormentors burn a question mark (not a cross) on their lawn. What a symbol, not just the flaming chalice but the flaming question mark. And we've probably all felt that burning need to know, to find out, explore, uncover new truths, new levels of understanding many times in our own spirits and minds and hearts.

We each have so many questions. Our human experience of living in the world guarantee that this will be so. And sometimes we don't want to live those questions. Sometimes we really want answers. And it is hard work. But it is work that gives purpose and meaning to our lives, true purpose and true meaning, because we have discovered it for ourselves.

to be patient to live the question
to live everything
to live the questions now....

We've also probably all learned how often answering one question leads to further questions. There's always more to learn. There's always more to wonder. There's always new knowledge, new understanding, new growth, new possibility, and there's always mystery. There's always mystery. Our lives are lived in that dynamic tension between knowing and not knowing. And either of these positions can inspire in us satisfaction, fulfillment, excitement, anxiety or fear.

For me, living in that dynamic tension between knowing and not knowing, challenges me to seek truth, to study, learn, stretch my mind, my heart and my spirit, and at the same time to accept and acknowledge the incompleteness of my knowledge and the mystery of much that is beyond my power to comprehend. It means that I must be open to feeling as well as thinking and open to experiences of awe and wonder and, yes, suffering that cannot be and need not be, put into words, yet can be appreciated and shared simply by being present to one another.

Knowing and not knowing. It's the human condition. In earlier times, people sought answers through magic and myths. Later, we tried to answer every question with science and reason. Now we are living in the age of technology. We're traveling the information super highway. But none of these things are answers. They are tools. They give us many ways to look at, think about, conceptualize, respond to, our questions. And they give us, yes, you guessed it, more questions!

Magic, science, technology, they do not answer what I consider to be basic questions of our human existence: Why must I die? And how, then, must I live?

Why must I die? Magic's response would be—you must die because you disobeyed the taboos of this culture. Science could describe the physical process of death. Reason could tell you the logic of life cycles. Technology could address the question of how shall I live by putting you on a respirator even if your brain and body can no longer function.

But the questions remain, and from these basics, all those other questions as well. And out of this need—this basic human need, this human cry, this human longing—religions have come. All kinds of religions—many forms—many expressions—but all developed or are developing in response to those basic human questions. All in response to that basic WHY? We have religions which claim to have the truth, own the truth, claim they are the one and only true religion. They have the dogma, the doctrine, the rules, the scriptures, the salvation. For some they are a safe harbor, for others, they are a prison.

Unitarian Universalism is a religion that developed in response to rigid dogma and exclusivity, a religion which stresses freedom with responsibility, which holds that revelation is not sealed, that we are all responsible to the interdependent web of all existence. For some, this is a community of liberation and hope. For others it would be an uncharted sea.

Those of us who choose Unitarian Universalism do so for a variety of reasons. But I would guess that all of us want a religion that will help us to bring our beliefs, our ideals, and our actions into increasing congruence and harmony. And we want this for our children as well.

We want to be able to question and doubt, to let go of outgrown, outworn beliefs and habits; to affirm those that are meaningful to us; to be open to new insights and understanding, to honor tradition when it is valuable to us, to widen and deepen our connectedness with others and the spirit of life and love, present in each of us yet greater than all, the spirit which I call God.

This God does not make bad things or good things happen. This God does not choose team A over team B in the playoffs, does not reward or punish, does not play favorites, is not exclusive to any group or denomination or nation, does not purposely rain or not rain on parade.

This God does not choose some people to be sick and others to be well, or some to be damned and some to be saved.

This God suffers with us. Weeps with us. Grieves with us. Laughs with us. Plays with us. Sings and dances with us. This God can be called by many names or by no name. But through this creative spirit of life, of love, of compassion, of justice, of mercy, of hope, which I am constantly discovering and learning and experiencing in my relationships and my connectedness with others. Through this interaction, this interactive God, I am learning the answers, bit by bit, to those basic human questions which inform my life. Why must I die? How, then, shall I live? We are the creatures who know we will die. But in that knowledge comes our appreciation, our valuing, of life.

You must answer this question. What will you do with your gifts? Choose to bless the world. The choice to bless the world can take you into solitude to search for the sources of power and grace, native wisdom, healing and liberation. More, the choice will draw you into community, the endeavors shared, the heritage passed on, the companionship of struggle, the importance of keeping faith, the life of ritual and praise, the comfort of human friendship, the company of earth, its chorus of life welcoming you. None of us alone can save the world. Together, that is another possibility waiting.

Recorded music: *The Unanswered Question* by Charles Ives, one of Lee's favorites.

CALL AND RESPONSE

When I was a child I lived with my family in or near Buffalo, N.Y. We moved several times during those growing up years and so I lived in several different neighborhoods in several different towns. There were some differences and many similarities. Though the style of houses might be different and the personalities of the people were different, some customs were remarkably consistent in every place I lived. One such custom, a ritual really, was the way we got together to play. When you wanted to see your friends when you wanted them to come out and play you called for them. Not on the phone. At the door. And never the front door. You went to the back door (or side door, where ever the not-front door was) and you called, like this: Mary! Mary! You didn't knock, or ring the doorbell you called, Mary! Mary! And Mary would come to the door and you'd say come on out. And she'd get her stuff whatever was needed and she'd come out. Then maybe just the two of you would play or maybe it was on to the next house to call Vivian or Margy and maybe then to call Richard or Tom.

Always the same way stand by the back door and call their name. I can hear it now. It's real to me. I can clearly remember standing there, calling to my friends to come out and play. And I can remember, too, being inside and hearing my friend's voice calling to me. Lee! Lee! Come out. Was it like that for you? Or maybe in your neighborhood you had a different way. Now, I guess it's a phone call. It's a play date. Every generation and every community probably has its own rituals. But I will never forget my first experiences of calling and being called. There was a connecting power there that was both real and symbolic.

Sometimes I wish it was still like that. Sometimes I wish I could stand outside your door and call: come out! come out and play! Of course you'd probably hear me and wonder what I was doing out there. Was there something wrong with me, standing there at your back door, calling your name? And what were you supposed to do about it? Invite me in? Call Wally to come and get me? Would you, could you come out and play? And would you ever come calling for me? And then, would we ever go together to call for another friend. Just picture it if you can.

Well, of course, we're not kids. We're grownups. And we have work to do. Schedules, Jobs, Deadlines. Today just isn't a good day for calling and response. Maybe some day, but not now. We're not kids, we're grownups. And no one is really going to come to our back door and call for us to come out.

And yet, and yet, something calls us. Something beyond phone calls and E-mail. Something beyond schedules and deadlines. Something beyond ego and perfectionism and guilt. Something calls us. Something calls us to love and service and creativity. Something calls us to come forth, come out of isolation, come out from behind the walls, come forth to a richer , fuller, more loving and hopeful life. Something calls us, has always called us, will always call us. It's a call of the spirit and it is real.

At one time or another all of us each of us reach dead ends in our lives. Find ourselves in times and conditions when we lose our joy, our passion, when we feel the languor of indifference or the rage of despair. Perhaps we don't know it, but in those hard times we are waiting (not even hoping, but waiting, nevertheless) for a CALL, the call to rise up, to come forth to LIFE.

Waiting to be called forth, as Lazarus from the tomb, not as a tricky miracle advertising some supernatural power, but called to come out of a dark and striking tomb of loneliness, despair, nothingness into a new vision of possibility, of hope and healing and connectedness. Waiting to be called forth, as dry bones from the lifeless valley called not just to individual life but called as a people a community united by the winds of the spirit as a force for love and justice in the world.

Within every person is the spirit—the Holy Spirit—of life and love. In everyone, somewhere, no matter how deep within, no matter how hidden, in everyone no matter how afraid, how angry, how bitter, how discouraged, how hurt, how weak, how worn, that holy, blessed, human, divine spirit lives. Hoping, praying waiting to be called forth, to be touched. To be embraced. To be known and loved and affirmed. It waits in you. It waits in me....

We are called, we are being called, to be callers. We are called, some of us as a minister, all of us as a ministering community, to respond to the calls, the cries of the spirit. We are called to reach out with words and song and acts of compassion, mercy and justice.

We are called forth as Lazarus from the tomb as dry bones from the valley of death
    not to an eternal party on the sky
    not to play our harps forever
    in the heavenly streets of gold

No!

We are called forth to a dream, a vision, a task larger than ourselves. We are called forth to live out the meaning of our lives, called forth to join our energies, our talents, our skills, our strength to join our spirits; our souls in the life work of building the Beloved Community right here, right now, every day. We are called to be chalices, flaming chalices burning with passion and compassion, chalices wide and deep enough to receive the pain and joy of all who hear and feel and respond to our call...

    all the dry bones,
    all who are entombed in loneliness; in the gloom
    of a flickering or dying hope,
    all who reach out, seeking companions, challengers,
    seeking to link life to life,

We are called to embrace all these and more. We are called to be open and vulnerable. To meet one another face to face, to tell the truth of our lives and LISTEN!

And most of all we are called to:
    love and love and love
    and not run away...
    love the pain and the struggle
    as well as the goodness and the beauty..
    love the tears as well as the laughter..

love and love and love
until our hearts break...
break open
break into a million aching, loving pieces..,
break and merge and beat together
in a drumbeat, a heartbeat,
a life beat of sisterhood and brotherhood.
the heartbeat that lies beneath all our diversity...
the heartbeat of unity which we are called to celebrate and share...
the unity of the web of all existence...
in which every person has worth and dignity...
the unity which calls us home to one another...
home to the arms of love.

CAN THESE DRY BONES LIVE?

R eading; from the book of Ezekiel:

The hand of the Lord came upon me, and He brought me out by the spirit of the Lord, and set me down in the middle of a valley. It was full of bones. He led me all around them, there were very many lying in the valley, and they were very dry. He said to me, "Mortal, can these bones live?" And I answered, "Oh Lord God, Thou knowest." Then He said to me,"Prophesy to these bones, and say to them, 'Oh dry bones, hear the word of the Lord.'" Thus said the Lord to these bones, "I will cause breath to enter you, and you shall live. I will lay sinews upon you, and will cause flesh to come upon you, and cover you with skin, and put breath in you and you shall live, and you shall know that I am the Lord.

So I prophesied as I had been commanded, and as I prophesied, suddenly there was a noise, a rattling, and the bones came together. Bone to it's bone. I looked, and there were sinews on them, and flesh had come upon them, and skin had covered them. But there was no breath in them. Then He said to me, "Prophesy to the breath. Prophesy mortal, and say to the breath, 'Thus says the Lord God, come from the four winds, oh breath, and breathe upon these slain that they may live.'" I prophesied as He had commanded me, and the breath came into them, and they lived, and stood on their feet, a vast multitude.

Ezekiel was a priest and a prophet of Israel, who according to the Hebrew bible, lived and prophesied 2500 years ago. He began his mission of prophesy during the last years of the kingdom of Judah, and at that time threats of destruction loomed closer and closer.

Destruction by corruption from within, and by the armies of the Babylonian empire, from without. Ezekiel saw the signs of the time. And in an effort to preserve and protect his people and their kingdom, he called on them to repent their selfish and evil ways, and he warned of the kingdom's impending downfall.

Despite his warnings, that is indeed what happened. And Ezekiel saw his people conquered by the invading Babylonian armies. Defeated and disbanded, many were exiled and taken away in captivity to Babylonia. Finally, Jerusalem was destroyed, and with it the temple in which the religious life of the entire people had been centered. His people, scattered, demoralized, their center gone, their faith shaken or denied, Ezekiel, ever the prophet, didn't give up. He saw to preach a new message, a message of hope and renewal, to find new ways to revive and maintain the traditions and values that lay at the heart of the Judaic experience. New ways to bind the scattered people together, so that the spirit of Israel would not die. Could these bones live? It was an important question then, at the time of defeat and exile those many years ago before the common era, and its an important question today, on our time, a time also of disarray and disconnection.

Now why, you may ask, am I talking about Ezekiel? Some say he was inspired, but some say he was just plain crazy, I'm talking about Ezekiel today because I do think he was inspired and I want all of us, each of us, to consider being Ezekiels in our own time. To enlist ourselves in what Unitarian Universalist theologian James Luther Adams has called the prophethood of all believers. In his book Taking Time Seriously, Adams writes, the prophetic, liberal church is the church in which all people think and work together to interpret the signs of the times in the light of their faith, with the intention of making history in place of being pushed around by it.

We are living in a time that demands and cries out for prophetic vision. Threats to all of life through war and the destruction of our environment. Threats to our psychological well being and our social structure. Economic oppression and polarization, racism, crime, drugs. These threats and the resulting feelings of powerlessness and alienation require us to find ways for people to experience community and to live more cooperatively.

Unitarian Universalism as an open, creedless faith with a tradition of concern and social responsibility can play an increasingly important part in building community and in celebrating unity in diversity. We can be prophets, creating a vision and imagery that people can understand telling the human story, the human dream in ways that will touch the human spirit.

The prophet Ezekiel has spoken to others over the centuries. Many, many years after the Babylonian captivity, African American slaves heard Ezekiel's story of the valley of the dry bones, and they, oppressed and denied their freedom, denied their very humanity, they identified with that story in a very special way. And they took Ezekiel's words, the story of hope and renewal, and they sang the words, they sang that story, and they made it theirs. Today, people who have never read the Bible know Ezekiel's story of the dry bones. They know the head bone connected to the neck bone, the neck bone connected to the shoulder bone, now hear the word of the Lord. People sing that song today because its fun to sing. But listen, think what that song is all about. Its about being connected, and about hearing the Word of the Lord. And for many Unitarian Universalists, they're one and the same thing.

Now, most of us would never use the term, Word of the Lord. For most of us, Lord is a sexist term. And for many of us traditional concepts of or words for God or Ultimate Reality simply don't apply. Yet we know there is as many ways as there are human beings to think about and speak about that Ultimate Reality. And many of us have also discovered that we can glimpse or experience this Ultimate Reality through our connections. When our head is connected to our heart, that we may become aware and think and feel and care. When our head and our heart are connected to our hands, that we may reach out to give, to receive, to embrace, to work, to create. When our head and our heart and our hands are connected to our feet so that we can act, move, stand up and be counted, go where we're needed, move along our life's journey. And when we are connected to each other, respecting and valuing every person. Listening to each other. Really being present for each other. And when we acknowledge our connectedness, our place, our part in the interdependent web of all existence.

It is in these experiences and of these experiences that I believe we must speak. We must find the words, inclusive words, words that invite rather than shut out. Words that are positive, rather than negative. Words that heal, rather than hurt. Words of truth and words of trust. Now I know its not easy to find the right words. We feel like the farmer who set out to buy a horse. He didn't have a lot of money to spend and he wanted to get the best horse he could. Well, he lucked out, he found a great horse, healthy, sturdy, good looking and at a very reasonable price. I'm selling him cheap, said his owner, because, because there's one unusual thing about him. If you don't mind that, he's a great horse. What's so unusual asked the farmer. Well, said the man was selling the horse, well, when you want this horse to go, you have to say, "Thank God." And when you want him to stop, you have to say, "Amen." "Well I can handle that," said the farmer, so he climbed on to ride him home. "Thank God," said the farmer, and the horse took off like the wind. Over the fields they raced, and finally they approached a deep, deep ravine. "Whoa," shouted the farmer, and the horse kept running. "Stop," the farmer shrieked. And the horse ran on. Just as they reached the edge of the ravine, the farmer remembered the right word. "Amen," he shouted and the horse came to a halt not one inch from the brink of the chasm. "Thank God," sighed the farmer.

We struggle to find the right words too, just like the farmer. What do we say when we feel so full of joy or of gratitude or praise, that we just need to shout it out. When we're so full of pain or grief that we need to cry out. When we're so full of good news about our chosen faith that we need to tell it, to share it. When we need to give voice to our religion, our spirituality, our deepest beliefs. To our yearning to welcome others, to invite them in, what do we say, and how do we say it? One of our most common definitions of Unitarian Universalism is, "Oh, if you're a Unitarian you can believe anything you want." You've heard that one. And we know what we don't believe. But that's not enough. When I was on the New York Metro District Extension Committee, I was asked to consult with a small Fellowship, concerned about its shrinking membership. They did a survey to find out what their members wanted or liked best about their society. And wine and cheese got the most votes. Religious and spiritual values got one vote. Now it's true that we experience community sharing wine and cheese. Sharing food can be a very powerful and meaningful religious experience, though we may not call it that.

The point is, that we need to articulate and share the underlying values that connect us and sustain us as well as the food that nourishes us so that people will be there to share the meal.

We need to celebrate the here and now, and also be clear about where we've been and where we're going. It's not easy. It's not easy to unpack religious language. It's not easy to accept responsibility to use language creatively, to find ways to say what we mean. To find out what we mean, so we can say it. It's not easy to look at where we've been, and where we're going while living fully in the moment. To do all that and to try and talk about it, that's asking a lot. But we can do it. When I was in seminary, a theology professor described liberal religion as a sort of artifact, something to be looked at in its historical content. Something of the past, something that is finished. It had gone as far as it could. The liberal religious mind had become so open, that everything fell out. I don't accept that definition. I believe that liberal religion is a positive, vital force in the world and can become through my efforts, through yours, even more so. I believe that the liberal religious mind can be opened to new insights, open to diversity, open to inclusivity, open to truth, not so open that everything falls out, but so that everything can fit in.

In the early nineteenth century, the great Unitarian, William Ellery Channing used the term, "liberal Christians." It was an inclusive term for those times when the orthodox Christian message was one of Hell and brimstone. Channing believed that everyone had the potential to do and be good and that human nature was capable of moving towards perfection. The orthodox religious right scorned the idea then, and they still do. Some say that liberal religion is worthless, is dead, because human nature has not been perfected. They still fight and kill, are angry, jealous, proud and lazy and that's true. However, this doesn't mean that human nature must be evil or that it doesn't make any difference. It means that we and every generation must define and articulate and strive for the best of human nature. And we must do this, knowing that we cannot succeed, not in the larger sense, for the orthodox were right. We will not make ourselves, or people or institutions or life, perfect. But that doesn't mean that our ideals and our visions are foolish. The very fact that we are able to conceive such ideals, glimpse such visions, and vision and yearn for greater wholeness, and share that vision, is inspiring. Unitarian Universalists, liberal religionists, are not the only people who believe these things.

But we are in a unique position to say them to people who might not hear. People who grew up feeling different, feeling like outsiders, who never quite fit in. People who have been told that they aren't the right color or the right sex. People who have been told that they don't have the right sexual orientation, or they don't have the right credentials. People with strong racial or ethnic ties to a religious community, but who can no longer accept the creed or the dogma or the teachings of that community. Couples of differing religions who want to build a shared religious life for themselves and their children, a life that respects and values the religious traditions of each. People who have been told not to ask so many questions. People who can't accept the official answers. People who want something more inclusive, more world embracing. People who revere more than one great tradition or teacher. People of other faiths who may never sign our membership books, but who want the exchange of ideas and wider understanding.

A new magazine called *American Prospect* has recently been started. Robert Reich, one of its founders, believes we are on the cusp of a new era. My simplistic vision, he says, is of a great emerging army of liberal people who don't have anything to attach themselves to. Reich is not talking about religious liberalism, but I think his words apply. And Hendrick Herzberg, editor of the New Republic said in response to Reich, "I think that when you get into one church, these independent voices that have been singing in different places will make a mighty chorus. I'd like to take his metaphor quite literally and apply it to Unitarian Universalism. I believe that we can make a mighty chorus. At our annual Unitarian Universalist General Assembly last June, the delegates gathered from UU societies all over this continent and voted unanimously to accept a ten year plan to promote and implement wider diversity within our denomination. After the vote was taken, the whole assembly broke into applause and cheers and smiles and tears. It was one of the most moving moments I've experienced in my many years of attending GA. And after our moments of elation came the inevitable question, how do we implement this historic vote, how do we give it flesh, make it real. Can these bones live? We will have to try and answer that question in many different ways. Each UU society exists in its own community, its own cultural context, has its own unique possibilities and limitations. But we can all put a high priority on communication, on exploring and learning about and valuing our differences and celebrating, lifting up, the areas that we share in common. Through worship, music, social action, and religious education, we can really try to be inclusive, what it means, what it takes and how and when it can happen. And we can be open to the enrichment and growth that openness to diversity can bring.

In the twenty-first century, what will our Unitarian Universalist Societies look like? I hope we are a lively, colorful group of people, drawn together by our commitment to freedom, truth, justice and love. Held together by friendship, caring, learning, by work and play. By our willingness to try, and by our willingness to have a dream and share that dream. By our willingness to stretch forth our hands and by our belief that other hands will be reaching out also. In the reaching, and in the touching, may we find what is truly holy and truly human. For together we have a message for the world, a message of healing, strength, freedom and hope. There are so many dry bones, parched, needing that message, needing to hear the words, words that will bring the waters of life, of refreshment, of renewal, to those dry bones so ready to hear. Are we ready to say those words? Can we find those words? Are we ready to shout them in enthusiasm, to whisper them in sympathy, to sing them in joy, to share them in grief? I believe we can, and I believe we must. Its our responsibility, its our task. To stand in the midst of the dry bones, and to reach out, and to speak our truth. You are lovable and worthy, each one—each one. The spark of life burns however weakly in each of us. We must nurture it, encourage it, share it, celebrate it. Say to the dry bones, you are a human being, with potential for good, and for evil. Choose good.

Let us join together in the struggle to find the good, and to choose over and over again. To gain, to lose, to love, to forgive, to keep trying, to keep alive and growing the faith and the hope and the love that sustain us, that we share. And that in the sharing reveals God in our midst, God the very act of struggle and sharing. Let's speak those words, and the dry bones will put on sinew and flesh and skin and rise up. And the words will be the breath of life and will animate us, so that our dry bones will be vulnerable, loving and struggling human beings, reaching out to each other in the dance of life. Con-nected, not just to a head bone to a neck bone to a shoulder bone to a hip bone, but connected to each other through the recognition of our humanness, to the vision of the possibility of growth and wholeness. The vision of human love, acceptance and passion and forgiveness. The unity of the human and the divine. Can these bones live?

Let us speak the words together, in truth and in love.

OUR DREAM OF RACIAL INCLUSIVENESS

Our topic for today, our dream of racial inclusiveness, is a big dream. Very big. It's shared by many people from all over the world. People of every race. But of course, as we all know, it is not shared by everyone. Racism is a world wide problem, a world wide threat, I believe, to human survival. As the world becomes more increasingly industrialized, as the world becomes more technological, our world's ecosystem becomes increasingly threatened, insulted, stressed, strained. And the world's people become increasingly threatened, insulted, stressed, strained.

We, the people of Planet Earth, need to learn better ways to understand each other, accept each other, respect each other, PUT UP WITH EACH OTHER, so that we can turn our full attention to the work that must be done to save our planet, save our world, .save, sustain, care for, LOVE this world, our home. We MUST do this. We cannot continue to pollute, exploit, waste, our natural resources, our precious resources, water, air, earth, energy, food, and people. The world is going to change. Change is inevitable. And we will each participate in that change, influence that change, by our actions. We know that. We know that we are a part of the interdependent web of all existence; that our lives, all lives, are inextricably bound together. We cannot run away from that knowledge. We cannot hide from our responsibility.

What can we do? We can make a commitment to be environmentally aware and responsible as possible, both in our personal lives and in our economic and political choices. And we can make a commitment to do whatever we can to promote understanding and harmony, equality and justice among people. These are the things that must be done and we are the people who must do them. It's as simple, and as complicated, as that!

We can support causes, vote wisely, contribute our money and our concern for global issues, national issues, local issues. There's so much to do! We can become overwhelmed just thinking about it all. But being overwhelmed won't do. Not at all. Being overwhelmed leads to the same results as passivity or indifference or copping out.

We know this. And so we make decisions about where we will put our time, our energy, our concern. We make choices about what we can and will do as conscious, aware citizens of the interdependent web. And some have chosen this Society, The Unitarian Universalist Society of the Palisades, as the place, or one of the places, where we will make a serious commitment. There are no doubt a variety of reasons why people join this society.

For some of us, a very high priority is our hope , our dream, of building a racially inclusive society, the larger society in which all people live and, as a first step, the smaller society that is Palisades. Some of us have a dream, a hope, a vision of how the world and its people might be. That is why we gather here, why we have made building this society such a high priority. I have a dream of racial justice, of racial equality, of a community, a world in which diversity is celebrated, respected, enjoyed, appreciated.

And I need to share my dream. I need companions, partners in the dream. So that when I am weary, when I am discouraged, when I make mistakes, when I am less than I should be, can be, when my light grows dim, you are there. You, with your light to guide me. Give me courage. Give me hope. Give me strength.

And I will do the same for you. My light will be renewed, and some day may help to light your path. We need each other, we who share a dream. We cannot build that dream alone. I came to Englewood because of my dream. I was contacted by representatives of the Unitarian Universalist Association, by our New York Metro District Executive and by the UUA Extension Department, which is in charge of starting new congregations and helping small congregations to grow.

They asked me to come to Englewood and try what they called a noble experiment, try to start and build a new Unitarian Universalist Society that would be racially inclusive. The idea was that if black people and white people could be partners from the start in building a new UU Society, we could create a congregation that would learn and grow as a model for what liberal religion wants and needs to be about.

We did not know if we could succeed, but the hope was that whatever else happened, we would learn, and that just by trying we would do something worth while; take at least a step towards our dream.

And I wanted to do this! Wanted it more than I wanted all the usual aspects of Unitarian Universalist ministry. I came to a strange new town where I knew no one. I had no church building, no congregation, no office, no help. None of the things I would have had if I'd gone to an established Unitarian Universalist congregation.

Nobody there to welcome us or bring us a casserole when we moved in. Nobody to stop by to see how we were doing. Nobody to show us the ropes or introduce us to their friends. Still, I wasn't alone. Wally, my husband, was still with me all the way. We also had 3 members from the old Rutherford UU society, which had dwindled away and was using its money to fund this new start.

But the hardest part was that I had no African American contacts and no entree into the community when I began my work in the Fall of 1988. However, shortly before we actually moved to Englewood, I met Lillian Thomas. She was going to tell this part of the story, but she is not able to do that. So I'll try.

A black couple, Gladys and Isaac McNatt, who live in Teaneck and attend the UU Community Church in NY City, heard of our endeavor and invited us to dinner at their house to meet with some of their black friends so they could learn about our society. At the dinner, I met Lillian Thomas, who no longer attended the McNatt's Church and had not attended any church for a long time. There was no immediate response. But I heard Lillian was in the hospital and I payed her a visit. I got to her when she couldn't resist and signed her right up! Now there was another person to share the dream, another little light to shine!

We began holding services here at Flat Rock Brook Nature Center in the Spring of 1989 and have since gathered a congregation of 50 people. More little lights! At time we've created quite a glow! Sometimes the glow gets pretty dim, though. But so far, when some of us fade, others are there to lift us up.

Of course, as could be expected, not everyone who comes here, not everyone who joins, shares the same dream, or has the same priorities. And that's OK. Unitarian Universalism seems to appeal most to people who are strongly individualistic, prize freedom and have little liking for authority, or authority figures, real or imagined.

However, this means that we have to be willing to give a good amount of our time and attention not only to the organization and operation of this society, not only to the programs and activities of this society..and believe me, these things need your help. But also we must give our time and attention to communication. We cannot assume that we all agree, or even that we are all aware of or care about the same issues. We cannot assume that we have the same dream or that we understand or interpret or prioritize the dream in the same way.

Therefore, we must talk together. We must share our dreams. We must share our various viewpoints and we must share our fears and concerns and hopes. We must always remember one simple truth: IF YOU DON'T TELL ME, I WON'T KNOW.

I am hoping that we will soon begin a series of informal meetings in which we can talk together about our hopes, fears, ideas and dreams for the future of this society. If we are to survive, we must be clear about why we want to survive. We must be clear about our mission, what it is we want and need to do, to be and to become.

Those of us whose priority it is to be an interracial society must share and articulate that dream. We must affirm ourselves as an inter-racial congregation which is truly inclusive and welcomes diversity of age, ethnicity, culture, sexual orientation, education and economic status.

I came here because of the opportunity and challenge of creating a racially diverse congregation. I also came here affirming that what-ever congregation we gathered would be the right congregation. Yet, to be truthful I would have to tell you that I would NOT have taken in the job of starting a congregation which intended or expected to be another white suburban upper middle class congregation. I can go and minister to a congregation like that and have a building, a secretary and other paid staff, a Sunday School of 100 and 300 adult members to share work and contribute pledges and invite me to dinner.

But I'm stubborn and opinionated, and I want to be a minister of a society that has a significant number of African American members, a diverse and inclusive congregation in every way possible.

I WANT THIS!

And the only way I could hope to get what I want was to come here and try to make it happen. Many of you have told me that this is what you want, too. Well, we've got to do more to make this dream come true. BECAUSE IF WE DON'T, WHO WILL? And if we do, then other groups can, too.

And as that happens, the world will become a better place. And future generations will bless us. Because we did what we could. We let our lights shine!

MOTHER'S DAY CELEBRATION

I know quite a few ministers who will NEVER preach a Mother's Day sermon or do a Mother's Day service. They feel that Mother's Day is just a sales gimmick, commercial manipulation of our emotions and sentiments by the retailing industry in order to sell more good, boost profits. I know quite a few lay people feel the same way that my ministerial colleagues do, Mother's Day is too commercial, let's not have anything to do with it.

I don't agree. I happen to believe that celebrating is very important in our personal lives and in our communities. And I think we should avail ourselves of every opportunity to do so. In our everyday lives we are subjected to a steady diet of bad news; disaster reports, crime stories and statistics, dire predictions of future troubles, economic woes, health warnings, child and spouse abuse; the list seems endless. If we read the paper, watch TV, listen to the radio, have almost any human contact, we will hear bad news. It overwhelms the good news and it can overwhelm us.

Now I don't believe in playing the Pollyanna. I don't believe in playing Dr. Pangloss, fervently insisting, evidence to the contrary, that "everything in the world is for the best in the best of all possible worlds." There is much bad news we must take seriously. There is misery; pain and injustice in the world, sometimes close to home, or in our homes. And we must pay attention and do what we can to relieve suffering, correct injustice, make things better. BUT to do this we must have a vision of possibility. To correct injustice we must be able to envision justice. To relieve suffering we must be able to envision healing and wholeness. To make things better we must be able to envision life, the world, as we want it to be. We must have faith and hope in the good, even as we acknowledge bad news.

This is why I believe we need to take every opportunity to lift up our ideals, our visions of good, not just in big, heroic events, but as they are lived out in our everyday, ordinary world. We need to do this as consistently and constantly as possible, but it's helpful to have reminders along the way. That's what holidays and special occasions provide. And I say, YES ! Let's celebrate them every chance we get. Let's remind ourselves that we have the right and the means and the creativity to celebrate Mother's Day, Father's Day, Valentines Day, Labor Day, Independence Day, and the big ones; Christmas and Easter, as OUR holidays. We don't have to let Hallmark or Macys or Victoria's Secret or the Religious Right or our own guilt and passivity define our behavior or impinge on our ability to celebrate as we see fit.

Now here's something else about celebrating: it doesn't mean sentimentalizing. Sentiment is good. We can be romantic, loving, poetic, MUSHY, CORNY, yes! BUT..we can also be truthful. We can celebrate not only what we have but what we hope for. We can celebrate joy while acknowledging pain. We can celebrate how far we have come and affirm how far we have to go. We can celebrate the tender times and the tough.

In other words, we can give our holidays the meaning and values we want them to have, and we can celebrate in ways that enrich and enhance our lives rather than trivialize and diminish them. And Mother's Day, today is one of those times when we can do just that. As far as motherhood is concerned, we all have one thing in common, we all had birth mothers. But from there on, our experiences have been many and diverse.

Some of us have had loving, nurturing mothering, whether from a birth mother or an adoptive mother. Some of us have not been so fortunate. Some of us may have been abused or neglected. We may not have received the tender loving care which we wanted and needed and deserved. Most of us, however, probably had mothers who did the best they could. And sometimes that best was pretty good, and sometimes it wasn't. Sometimes the mothering was right on target, and sometimes it wasn't. We didn't always get what we needed and we certainly didn't always get what we wanted.

Most of us here today probably feel that motherhood should be a choice. We believe that each woman should have the right to make that choice for herself. Ideally, this choice would be made in conjunction with a loving life-partner, and both would want and nurture the child and help and support each other as parents. As we all know, this is not always possible. There are accidental pregnancies. Single women choose to have a child. Parents split up. A woman may not have the physical, emotional or economic resources necessary to be an adequate parent. Mothering is extremely difficult to do alone. It is difficult when there are partners.

Let me read to you an excerpt from a column by Linda Weltner in *Boston Globe*:

> Poor mom stands alone. Against merchandisers who sell faddish clothes and expensive possessions as an essential ingredient of the good life. Against the $400 million spent annually on advertising campaigns directed at children. Against inflation, which threatens family security, and pollution, which poisons it. Against cut-rate schools and drugs and the influence of her children's peers. The fact is that too often the mother who is labeled neglectful or rejecting is simply overwhelmed.
>
> Supportive husbands, good schools and safe neighborhoods are in short supply. So are understanding bosses, helpful neighbors, and extended families. Home is no longer a sanctuary from the forces at work outside it, and no one knows that better than the mothers who are often held responsible for the harm their children sustain.
>
> After all, who else is in charge of nurturing in this culture? Who else is expected to be unconditionally loving and patient and self-sacrificing except Mom? I'm deliberately leaving Dad out of this, because even a mediocre father is likely to be given credit for his efforts by the same children who take the mother's attention for granted.
>
> "Because we have higher expectations for mothers than for fathers, we are quick to criticize our mothers for not being perfect, but appreciate our fathers for merely trying," says psychologist Paula Caplan in her eye-opening book, *Don't Blame Mother*. "Mother blaming is so pervasive that it's almost a wonder that women choose to become mothers ," she goes on to say. We compare our mother to the "perfect mother" and find her wanting. We see mother's strength in comparison to our smallness and never come to understand how uncertain and powerless she may have actually felt. We hold her responsible at 50 for the things she did at 20. And even when we become mothers and struggle with

the same difficulties ourselves - isolation, exhaustion, a sense of inadequacy, feelings of guilt and fear of failing - we have trouble shifting from our childish perspective.

Paula Caplan's book is about learning to let go of all that. Maybe the best thing to do on Mother's Day is to realize how sad it is that motherhood can come between women who should be natural allies - mothers and their daughters - and in some way reach across the generations to say, "I understand how hard this job is."

And if we have unresolved negative feelings about our mothers we will carry them over into our own mothering. We may fear we'll make the same mistakes and so we go to the opposite extremes to avoid them. We may feel that our children are judging us as we judged our mother, and that we, too, will be found wanting. We may try so hard to be perfect parents that we and our children will live with great stress and tension.

We did not - do not - have perfect mothers.
We will not - are not - perfect children.
We are not perfect parents.
And our children aren't perfect either.

Children need people who care for them, and so do adults. We never grow out of that need, the need to be in caring, respecting, right relationship with others. We all need to be loved unconditionally, just as we are, with no need to win love or prove love, no need to be judged. We need to give that kind of love, too. We all have times when we need to be comforted, hugged and held close. We all have times when we need someone to believe in us so that we can believe in ourselves. We all need to develop our ethical and moral values and standards, and we can't do that all alone.

And that's what I think Mother's Day is, or can be, all about. Celebrating motherhood in all its truths, its imperfections and needs, its moments of love and tenderness, the frustration, the humor, the work and the play. We don't have to go to the candy store or the florist or Victoria's Secret, but we can if we want to, if it feels good rather than bad. We can make our own traditions, recognize old ones or start new ones today. We can share our thoughts and ideas about how to make this a truly meaningful celebration for all, and about all, children, mothers, parents, families.

I don't want to gloss over some of the problems that some children face. There are inadequate parents, abusive parents. Ignorant or selfish or irresponsible parents, missing parents. Some of us today may have had very painful or destructive experiences. I hope not. And society at large provides inadequate response and support for families in need, especially single parent families. Children and mothers make up the largest percentage of our poorest people and they are increasingly being scapegoated and victimized by the Radical Right and by political opportunism and indifference.

My wish is that we as a society will give increasing support, education and counseling to all mothers, all parents. I hope for the day when all families will have decent, affordable housing and childcare. When employers will find more creative ways for parents to have jobs and families and do justice to each. When mothering is respected and valued as important work. When children are appreciated and cared for as our most precious resource.

My wish is that we will explore ways in which we as individuals and as a congregation can support each other and the larger community in nurturing families, including helping one another, volunteering in the community, getting active politically in supporting legislation for day care, health care and education. And we can provide a welcoming, safe and nurturing place where children and adults, all of us, can learn and grow in understanding and wisdom, courage and compassion, goodness and grace. May all our celebrations lead us to love.

And now, as our special Mother's Day sharing time, I invite you to light a candle for someone you honor as a mother, a mentor, a nurturer. You may do this in silence or with words if you prefer. After you light a candle, please take a carnation, also in honor of motherhood. In the tradition of the Black church, a red carnation honors mothers who are living and a white carnation honors mothers who have died.

I light this candle for my mother, Laura Morrissey, 90 years young, a role model of courage, love and humor. For her, the glass is always more than half full, and meant to be shared. I love her dearly.

We are thankful for the love and care we have received. May our ability to love, to give and to understand be strengthened and deepened.

FAMILY VALUES

Well, as you know, our topic this morning is family values. Can you stand to hear that phrase just one more time? The Republicans sought to make it a major focus, an issue of their campaign this year and they set about to instruct us all as to the proper definition or understanding of the term. Good, right family values means traditional family values: two parents of the opposite sex, married, with children, all living together. The father works and supports the family, the mother stays home and takes care of the family. The children go to school, they stay out of trouble, and they grow up to emulate their parents and create another generation with traditional family values. Now, I think this is a fine model of a family, but unlike the family values crowd, I don't think it is the only model. It's just one of the varieties of family that populate our country and our world today. And I don't like the idea that a group of politicians or clergy or anybody else thinks they can co-opt words and concepts like family and values and force them into one restrictive mode.

I don't like that at all. I don't like it that family and values have become code words for racism and sexism or any other ism. And I don't like it that family values is being made to mean stereotyping of the roles of both men and women. And I don't like it that family values is being made to mean no abortion, restriction of information about contraception, the gag rule. I don't like it that family values is being made to mean that single parents, in particular single mothers, are somehow wrong or bad or unworthy of respect and support. I don't like it that family values is being made to mean that same sexed couples can't legally be a family, have no rights as a family. And I don't like it that the definition of family values separates and divides people rather than bringing them together. I'm not willing to leave the definition and the ownership of family values to a self-selected group of negative and self righteous people. So, folks, by the power invested in me as a Unitarian Universalist minister I claim family values as open, inclusive, wide-ranging and affirming. That's why it's nice to have power.

Now, we've all heard the response to the rigid discrimination which defines this year's political usage of the term family values. It's this: family values is about valuing family. And this is true and I want to talk about that with you later, but first, let's ask a very basic question. What is a family? We've described the traditional family: mother, father, children all living together; father works outside the home and supports the family; mother works inside the family and takes care of the family; children, yes, emulate the parents, they repeat the story, but they should be even more successful because it's onward and upward forever. The traditional family is the nuclear family. But ideally this traditional family should have connections to a larger family with grandparents and aunts and uncles and cousins. And the family is bound together by religion, by race, by ethnicity, by class and by economic status and by a shared value system.

Until quite recently, this definition of the traditional family very much dominated our American society's perceptions and procedures and practices. Single parenting was acceptable only for those who were widowed. Divorce was frowned upon. Parents were to stay together, to make every effort to stay together for the sake of the children. Couples were not supposed to live together unless they were married and certainly we all know that the single woman who dared to have a baby, whether by intent or by surprise, was considered to be a very fallen kind of woman and for generations those children were called illegitimate, were called bastards, were not often allowed to inherit. This was a very bad thing to do. But, that was then, and this is now. And I'm wondering, how to we define a family today? The dictionary (I always go to the dictionary when I think of definitions) says all the traditional things: it's parents and children, it's all the descendants of a common ancestor, it's a group of things that are alike in some way. And that's about as far as they go in defining a family.

If any of you read the op-ed page of the *New York Times* yesterday, perhaps you read the little article by James Stockdale II, who was very upset about the role that his father had to play and was assigned to play in the vice presidential debate. He wrote something that I thought was very interesting. He gave us his definition of a family and this is what he said: a family is any group of loving people mutually willing to put unity over self. M. Scott Peck in his book *The Road Less*

Traveled, which many of you've probably read, defines love as the willingness to expand and extend my boundaries for the sake of nurturing my own and another's spiritual growth. So looking at these two definitions we might say that a family would be people who nurture their own and each other's spiritual growth and are willing to put unity over self. Now, I think I would define unity here as connectedness and self as isolated ego. And so there we would say again that a family would be people who are united in love for each other's mutual spiritual growth and well being. That seems like a pretty good definition.

But does a family have to be a group? Does it have to be people living together? I think sometimes it's very difficult for single people to come to gatherings and always hear about family services, family values, doing things as a family, and can be a very isolating feeling when you live by yourself. Sometimes you can feel excluded from all those family events and definitions.

What I would like to do with you now instead of just having a sharing time at the end, is to consider some types of families and what you think a family might be. Let me start by saying I began thinking of all the different kinds of people that I know and the different kinds of families that I see them involved with and creating and sometimes pioneering with as we move on towards the end of this century. I'm thinking of some one that I know who lives alone and yet feels a part of a family because this person has connections with another and much younger couple whose own parents are dead. And this woman has made strong bonds with this young couple that she met and really has created her own family, maybe not by birth, maybe not by blood, maybe not a genetic family, but a family nevertheless by our definition of people united in love and concern for each other's spiritual well being. And it's wonderful to see this relationship and how it works and how it benefits all three of these people: one 87 year old woman, and two younger people in their forties who have as much of a bond, I think, as any of us could have as parents or children.

I'm thinking of other kinds of families, too. I'm thinking about a woman that I know who made the decision to have her daughter and her son-in-law come and live with her, who then had two children and now they are what is called a multi-generational family: grandmother, parents, granddaughter, baby grandson, living together, working out their difficulties because it's not always easy to live one generation with another or a mother to live with a daughter, and yet working it out very well and enjoying the experience. I've watched this family develop and now I see that this older woman has become quite ill and quite frail. I wonder sometimes what it would be like if she hadn't made these kinds of connections and was now in a nursing home somewhere with children who would come to visit once in a while, which is often what happens. But in her case she was fortunate enough to work a long time to make a relationship that now is sustaining her when she really needs it. I'm thinking also of other kinds of families. One parent. How about some more kinds of families. Perhaps you'd like to describe your own. A family that is a family but maybe not the traditional family we described today.

THEOLOGICAL REFLECTIONS ON THE LITTLE RED HEN

When I ask who knows the story of the Little Red Hen, my sermon title, most people immediately respond with "The sky is falling...the sky is falling." But that's the story of Henny Penny, a story for another day. The Little Red Hen is different:

A little red hen was in the farmyard with her chicks, looking for something to eat. She found some grains of wheat, and she asked:

" Now who will help me plant the wheat?"

"Not I," said the duck. "Not I," said the mouse. " Not I," said the pig.

Then I'll plant them myself," said the little red hen. And she did. When the grain had grown tall and was ready to cut, the little red hen asked:

"Now who will help me cut the wheat?"

"Not I," said the duck. "Not I," said the mouse. " Not I," said the pig.

"Then I'll cut it myself," said the little red hen. And she did. When the wheat was cut, the little red hen then asked:

"Now who will help me thresh the wheat?"

"Not I," said the duck. "Not I," said the mouse. " Not I," said the pig.

"Then I'll thresh it myself," said the little red hen. And she did.

When the wheat was threshed, the little red hen then asked;

"Who will help me carry the grain to the mill?"

"Not I," said the duck. "Not I," said the mouse. " Not I," said the pig.

When the wheat was ground, the little red hen then asked:

"Who will help me bake the bread?"

"Not I," said the duck. "Not I," said the mouse. " Not I," said the pig.

"Then I'll bake it myself," said the little red hen. And she did.

When the bread was baked, the little red hen said:

"The bread is done! Now who will come and help me eat it?"

"I will," said the duck. "I will," said the mouse. "I will," said the pig. And they came running.

"No you won't!" said the little red hen, and she called to her chicks. "Come, my chicks. I planted the wheat, cut and threshed it, and carried it to the mill. I baked this bread for you. Now eat it up! Eat it up!"

And they did

I came upon this story from my childhood just a few years ago in a Unitarian Universalist Sunday School curriculum we were using. The story was used to spark a classroom discussion about our interdependence, how it takes work and cooperation of many people to supply our needs, and our wants. But when I learned the story as a child I never heard about interdependence. No. I always heard that the moral of this story was: No work, no eat. There you have it, a simple, straightforward, all American, homespun moral, no work, no eat.

Except, of course, in the version of the story (the version I just read you) where the Little Red Hen has chicks and they get to eat the bread even though they haven't done the work. They are young and dependent and they are the Little Red Hen's children, her responsibility.

Well, any how, the Little Red Hen does all the work and she gets rewarded. She and her chicks get all the bread. She isn't seen as selfish because she doesn't share the bread with the other animals, the non-helpers. She is seen as virtuous. And the barnyard animals who wouldn't help, they are seen as the selfish ones, and the get their comeuppance, no bread for them. No work, no eat.

This story illustrates a simplistic, wishful thinking view of human interdependence. Everyone works and everyone shares the fruits. Everyone participates and everyone benefits. And society is pretty clear about defining work and participation and rewards. Our economy is based on no work, no eat. But it has also been based on exceptions to the rule. If you can't work because there are not enough jobs or you have no skills or training or you are too old, too young, too sick or disabled, or have children to care for, then those who have more than enough, who have jobs or professions or inheritances, share with you according to their means, through taxes, through charity, through volunteerism.

If this worked perfectly, the richer people got, the richer all people would get. But in fact, we know that this is not the case. We are told that, instead, the gap between the rich and the poor is widening, that the middle class is becoming increasingly fearful, that there is very little feeling of connectedness or interdependence, and that there is a great deal of resentment, anger, guilt and despair.

No work, no eat, the politicians cry, as their constituents, in increasing numbers, face the once unthinkable possibility of economic downsizing and financial insecurity and in their fear and anger and disappointment they make scapegoats of the poor and the least able. The new politics is a politics of scarcity..."There's not enough to go around, so I'm certainly not sharing any with you! So you have no jobs or skills or training or you're too old or too young or too sick or too disabled, too bad. No work, no eat!"

What's going on here? Of course there's economic injustice, grave injustice. But that's nothing new. Of course there are too many poor people. But that's nothing new. Of course there are greedy corporations and a lack of corporate responsibility. But that's nothing new. Of course our welfare system and our social service systems don't work very well, but that's nothing new.

What's new, I think, is this scarcity mentality, the growing fear, belief, that there's just not enough to go around. And I believe that this scarcity mentality is not just about money per se. It's about scarcity of love and acceptance and caring and respect. It's about the very real fear that there's not enough to go around. It's about the apathy and cynicism that come with scarcity thinking.

What's going on here?
What can we do?

Perhaps one way we can begin to understand the world situation and the national situation is to consider our own personal situations. We all suffer at times from the Little Red Hen syndrome. We feel that we are doing more than our share and others are doing less. We feel used or martyred, resentful or envious, we feel alone, disconnected. We share no common goal, or no one seems to share our goal.

And that's an important point. The fact of the matter is that those who share a common vision share a common goal and can be partners in the process rather than competing or just being indifferent to one another. The Little Red Hen saw the possibility of bread in those few grains of wheat, she could almost smell it, taste it, she new how good it would be.

As the wheat grew,as she weeded the grain and harvested it and had it milled. The bread became more and more possible, more and more real. Every effort on her part brought the bread nearer. Finally, she baked the bread, and there it was! Delicious, fragrant, sending out that mouth-watering aroma. When the other animals actually smelled the bread, then they were ready to enjoy and appreciate it. They hadn't shared in the original vision or planning, so the process seemed pointless. Only when they saw the product could they start to connect.

Life's like that. Those who share the same vision will share the goals and the process, will work together to make that vision a reality. Those who, for a variety of reasons, don't or can't share in that vision, simply won't, can't, have the same level of commitment.

Of course, even among those who share a common vision, there will be a variety of ways of working to make it real. People enjoy work the most when they can work from their strengths. However, not all work is fun and some is downright unpleasant. The shared vision make that work possible, do able, keeps us going. And if our common effort helps to make the vision increasingly clear, then, along the way, more people may be able to see it, share it, and join the process.

TO BE OF USE

I want to be with people who submerge
in the task, who go into the fields to harvest
and work in a row and pass the bags along,
who are not parlor generals and field deserters
but move in a common rhythm
when the food must come in or the fire be put out.

The work of the world is common as mud.
Botched, it smears the hands, crumbles to dust.
But the thing worth doing well done
has a shape that satisfies, clean and evident.
Greek amphoras for wine or oil,
Hopi vases that hold corn, are put in museums
but you know they were made to be used.
The pitcher cries for water to carry
and a person for work that is real.

a poem by Marge Piercy

As we face the challenge of how we can work together to build a better, kinder, more humane society, to build a new world order. It might be helpful to consider how we can do this on a smaller scale as we work to build our families, our friendships and our religious and spiritual communities.

For example, we know that as partners or families, we need to have a shared vision, a shared commitment, to that partnership or family. It's not enough to focus on what I as an individual want from the relationships, or even what I can give to the relationships. We need to share with each other our vision or what partnership or family is all about. Our commitment is to the totality, not just a piece of it. Our needs will change. The relationships will change, but the partnership, the family, endures.

Another example: We have embarked on a mission to build a new, diverse, welcoming Unitarian Universalist Society. It takes a huge amount of effort and commitment to start a new society from scratch as we are attempting to do. And each of us has our own level of commitment, list of priorities, needs and expectations. But unless building this new UU society is very, very high on some people's priority list, unless commitment of a really major amount of time and energy is made by some of us, this society won't be here for any of us. Unless some of us are willing to do much more than our share, this society will not survive.

And unless the most committed people reach out to invite and inform and empower others to grow in commitment, grow into leadership, unless all of us do our best to cooperate and support one another, to nurture one another, this society will not become all it can be.

That is how life lis on every level. Like it or not, every creation takes major effort. And we have to really watch out for the Little Red Hen syndrome. No one of us can or should take on the vision or the goal alone. It must be shared, you can't build a community or a society, small, large or world-wide, any other way. If I, for example, your minister, or any of us ever feel I've become the Little Red Hen, or if others assign us that role, we are in trouble. If the refrain ever begins to be "Not I," or "Then I'll do it myself," watch out. We're done for.

Well, it all can seem pretty overwhelming. If it's that difficult to build a small society like ours, how can we ever expect to build a nation and a world society of peace and justice? Faith, hope, love and a sense of humor. Keep on believing, keep on communicating, keep on talking, keep on listening, reach out, hold hands, keep the connections strong, and practice, practice. And folks, there's no other way, do the work that only you can do, and know you make a difference.

Don't be like the barnyard animals who said "not I, not I." Pay attention, get involved in the process. Don't be like the Little Red Hen who could only say, "Very well then, I'll do it myself." Reach out. Share the vision. Keep inviting. Don't give up. If only the Little Red Hen had been able to get together with the other animals right in the beginning, and together they could have decided what to do with those grains of wheat.

There's a lot we don't know about this story, about why the other animals weren't interested in helping, about the power and control and passive aggression and workaholism and what other food was available. But this was just a little story written to teach a lesson. Trouble is, nothing's simple. Still, I'm glad our children who hear this story in UU Sunday School will learn about interdependence and caring, learn that there's more to it than no work, no eat. May they grow up better able to share the vision of peace and justice and make it real.

At one time we used to say and believe, "Give me a fish and I eat for a day, teach me to fish and I eat for a lifetime." We know this isn't enough; we must also make room at the pond. There are still those people in the world whose only hope is that we the powerful will be humble and merciful and just.

As Wolves See It:
Truth and Reality

D r. F. Forrester Church wrote, in his book *The Seven Deadly Virtues*:

You may be interested to know that the wolves have a different version of Little Red Riding Hood than we do. It's not all that surprising really. The meaning of the story and even its details change according to the perspective of the one who is telling it. This is true of everything from Custer's Last Stand to the four holy gospels. In any event, as a scholar might phrase it, here is the lupine reduction of the Riding Hood tale.

Once upon a time there was a good wolf, always helpful to others, always kind. One day, when walking through the woods on his morning constitutional, he encountered a little girl dressed all in red. At first he was frightened because humans have a history of being cruel to wolves, but he overcame his fear and welcomed her to his part of the woods.

"Where are you going, little girl?" the kind wolf asked. "To my grandmother's house on the other side of the forest," the little girl replied. "My grandmother is very old and very ill, and I am taking her this picnic basket filled with treats to make her young and well again."

What a sweet little girl, thought the wolf to his self, yet so naive, so unschooled in the ways of the woods, which are the ways of life and death. The more he pondered this, the more worried he became. Perhaps he should have accompanied the little girl, not just to protect her from any who might wish her harm, but also gently share with her a little of his wisdom, lest, as children often do, she would end up feeling in some way responsible when her grandmother died.

By this time the little girl had quite a head start. Nonetheless, the good wolf put down his walking stick and ran as fast as he could to the little girl's grandmother's house, taking a shortcut he knew, hoping perhaps to accompany the little girl, during which time they could discuss these things at leisure.

When he arrived at grandmother's house, the wolf knocked on her door, unsure as whether or not the little girl had already arrived. There was no answer. He knocked again. Still no answer. The door was unlatched so he entered the cottage, only to discover the little girl's grandmother lying lifeless in her bed. She had no pulse and was not breathing. Desperately, he attempted artificial respiration, but to no avail. He could not resuscitate her.

Just then he heard the little girl singing sweetly in the distance as she approached the cottage. Determined to protect her from the shock of finding her grandmother dead, he had to think fast. Then it struck him. He had one chance, albeit a risky one. Though he had already enjoyed a good breakfast and was not hungry at all, he wolfed the old woman down, threw on her nightgown, and jumped under the covers.

Despite the wolf's best intentions, as so often happens, everything went wrong that possibly could. To begin with, his disguise was far from perfect. When the little girl came in, her curiosity concerning her grandmother's appearance let her to ask a number of questions, about the length of her nose, for instance, and the depth of her voice, but when she commented upon the size of her grandmother's teeth and the wolf replied as sweetly as possible, " The better to eat with, my dear" (prejudice later added the "you"), the little girl recognized that this was not her grandmother at all, screamed and ran from the cottage. The good wolf pursued her, trying to explain, but before he had a chance, a hunter leapt from the underbrush and shot him dead.

Very sad.

Wolves love to hear this story, I am told. Around the den at night time, when Daddy and Mommy tuck the cubs into bed, it is the one they usually ask to hear, even though they know it by heart. The moral never fails to move them. Even though the good wolf was killed, in a way he died for all wolves, for through the example of his life generations of wolves have been inspired to perform unself-regarding deeds of kindness.

Who is this wolf, anyhow? The Hero Wolf? The Victim Wolf? The Martyr Wolf? The Big Bad Wolf? You know, I heard the Story of the Three Little Pigs and the Story of Little Red Riding Hood nearly all my life, since I was a very small child, and it was always poor little pigs and poor little Red Riding Hood and always the Big....Bad....Wolf. Nobody ever asked the wolf to tell his story. It never occurred to us that the wolf had a story to tell!

But, as dear old granny often use to say, there are at least two sides to every story. Every hero is a villain to somebody. One person's victim is another person's passive aggressor. A person revered as a martyr by some will be denounced as a charlatan by others. All people in positions of leadership, in public office or in the public eye know this. And, in greater or lesser degrees, all of us have struggled with issues of credibility, differences in perception, varieties of viewpoints. All of us have struggled to understand and define our concepts of truth and illusion, fact and opinion, reality and fantasy.

We want the truth. Ah, but the question is, whose truth? The wolf, the hunter, Little Red Riding Hood, the grandmother. The three little pigs. Each one had the true story. Yet each story would be different. We each tend to see what and how we've been taught to see. If we've been taught that wolves are bad and mean and we have to get them before they get us, that's what we'll probably believe. That's what the hunter believed, so he killed the wolf. But gee, wolves are dangerous. That's the truth. If I met a wolf in the woods, I'm certainly not going to walk up to it and pet it. Or even just stand there and smile and say "nice wolf." So what am I supposed to do?

Well, the truth is, unlike Little Red Riding Hood, I don't think I'm ever going to walk in a woods where wolves live. I'm never going to suddenly meet one face to face. Still, I can check out my perception that wolves are bad and mean people, killers. If I do that, I'll find that there are a lot of differing opinions about wolves. I can also find out some facts. I can find out about their physical characteristics and their behavior as observed and recorded by naturalists. I can get statistics on what they eat and how many people are known to have been killed or eaten by wolves. Those are facts.

I can also learn that some say wolves should be killed because they eat too many other animals and some say we should leave it up to nature to keep things in balance. Those are opinions. After I find out what I can about wolves, when I've learned the facts and heard different opinions, then I will make up my own opinion. And I will have to accept that everyone won't agree.

Where's the truth then? The truth is in acknowledging that I am responsible for my opinions and so must be well informed. The truth is in acknowledging that everyone won't agree, but that doesn't absolve me from my responsibility to do my best to learn and try to understand and issue, or a person, or a wolf and to be open to new insights and learning.

Sometimes we don't realize that everyone doesn't see things as we do. Some things seem so obvious, so certain to us that it would never even occur to us that there could be another way of seeing. I heard a story one time about an airline pilot whose little son often came to the airport to wave goodbye as his daddy's plane took off. So when daddy decided to take his little son with him on a flight to Florida, he expected that the little boy would be happy and excited to finally be on a plane with his dad. Instead, the child sat tense and nervous as the plane took off.

"What's the matter, son?" the father asked as the plane climbed into the sky. "Daddy," the little boy whispered, "Daddy, when are we going to get smaller?" From his experience and viewpoint, when planes took off they and everyone in them got smaller and smaller as they got further away. Who would know that's what he'd think and fear, and yet from his perspective, the fear was real and his expectations perfectly logical.

Sometimes we have no idea how what we say can be interpreted by someone else. We know we are making sense, but what a surprise it is sometimes to find out what the other person has heard. Wally reminded me of a conversation between two children who were discussing household chores. "What I hate the worst is washing the dishes," said one. I sneak upstairs and hide so maybe my mom won't make me do them. "I have to do the dishes," said the other kid. "It's part of our religion." "It's part of your religion?" "Yeah, my mom always yells at me and says 'For Christ's sake, do those dishes!'"

There's always been debate over whether truth is absolute or relative. This has always been a strong component of religion. Most religions teach that they have the truth. With a capital T. I remember a bumper stickers of the 1970's that read, I've found it. Unitarian Universalists put one out that read I'm still looking. But, as you know, most Christian denominations have a creed, a list of things you have to believe in if you want to be a member. Some believe that the Bible is the source of all truth. Some even teach that you must believe every word in the Bible. That's a lot or words! And many of them contradict each other.

But these people, Biblical literalists, say there is no contradiction, every word is true, once you understand their version of what is written. And that's the truth! Others aren't quite so literal but they still think that their interpretation of the Bible and their rules, based on that interpretation, are based on absolute truth and everyone should agree. Wars have been fought over whose truth is the true truth. People have been persecuted and martyred. It still happens today. One of the most important things about Unitarian Universalism, for me, is that we say that nobody has all the truth. No book, no religion no leader. We say there is always more to learn. We should never stop asking questions and doing our best to learn more. We each, for example, are on our own individual spiritual journey, spiritual quest. The reason we are here is to conduct our quest in the company of seekers, to have companions on the journey. This is good. However, we cannot expect, or require, that others affirm/accept our journey, our path, our needs, as the way, the truth. We cannot demand or expect that our personal religious journey; our spiritual path, be the only way. We can't say of our personal journey: My way or the highway.

We say that we can learn from each other and that when we come together with different viewpoints we don't have to fight. Well, we surely can discuss. But we can do it with respect and with a willingness to really listen to what others have to say. And we can expect respect for our own ideas too, even it they aren't just like everyone else's. Some say that's not so easy. Sometimes we aren't really so sure what we think and that's OK. Just as we each see things differently at times, so sometimes we see one way and sometimes another.

Sometimes, though, we see things that aren't really there. We may think they are, or we may think they should be, so after a while it seems that's the way it really is. Sometimes people can get really caught up in this, and believe that because they say something with great fervor or conviction, it's really true. The lines between fantasy and reality become blurred and broken. Sometimes this is deliberate. It's called a lying. We lie to get our own way, to make ourselves look good, to make others look not so good. We lie to avoid blame, we lie out of envy, fear, guilt, or a need for power and control.

Sometimes we lie because we don't want to hurt someone's feelings. Because we want someone to like us. Because we don't want to cause trouble. A lot of times we don't mean to lie. But we do. We just sort of exaggerate. Get carried away. Dramatize. Embroider. Flesh it out. It's bad enough when we do this with our own story, but it's worse when we do this about someone else. When we interpret someone else's story, add our own opinions and judgements, without being clear about what we are doing. And oh, that's so easy to do. So easy. Sometimes we don't even realize what we're doing. We just get caught up in the story, in the telling of it. Even it's not our story to tell.

Each person has the task, as a responsible member of society, of monitoring our own behavior and speech. When we become passionate or enthusiastic or angry about an issue, an idea or a person, we may voice, or even promote, our opinions and feelings as facts, as the truth. We can undermine or severely damage a person and/or the group, the community, in this way. Whether or not that is our conscious intention, the results are the same. We tear down rather than build up. Some people learn to depend on this sort of behavior in order to feel important. It becomes a way of relating to others. It's called triangling, allying oneself with another person at the expense of the third person. It can be done very self-righteously:

"I think the world of Caroline, but..."
"We all love Joe, but..."
"I don't mean any disrespect, but..."
"I only want what's best for   . (add, everyone, or the society...)

And with such a pious, caring, opening, the person goes on to trash the other person or group. Gossip, rumor and innuendo can destroy. And all in the name of good intention, all in the name of truth. We have seen the results of this behavior in the political arena.

Opinion càn be swayed. Votes can be solicited. Elections can be won. But the price in the long run is disillusionment, distrust and apathy. The price is destruction, often of the very thing that was intended to be lifted up; often, unfortunately, of a reputation, a career, or a good and worthy cause.

Another destructive practice is exaggeration. The person finds one or two others who agree with his or her opinion, or perhaps, simply they don't actively disagree, or challenge that opinion. That's all some people need to feel affirmed in stating their case:

"There's a feeling in the group that..."
"A group of us all think that..."
"The prevailing opinion is..."
"I am not alone in wanting..."
"We all know that...."
"Many of us feel that..."

Human beings love to tell stories. We have a burning need to communicate, to connect, to share our thoughts and feelings and experiences. It's so important to us that we've invented language, millions of words, that weave us together in the interdependent web. Yet even with all those words communication can be difficult, frustrating, challenging. Because although we are all part of the interdependent web, each of us has our own unique place, and so each viewpoint, each perspective, is unique. No one else will ever see the world exactly as we do. That is the glory and the agony of being human.
But we try. We must try to tell our own stories, to listen and learn the stories of others, and to do this with as little distortion as possible. Of course, because we are not-quite-yet-perfect human beings, and because we live in community, we talk to and about one another. We gossip, yes, we all do, at least occasionally. We try to present ourselves in ways that will gain attention, affection, admiration! We tend to look for somewhere else to put the blame. We can be careless or thoughtless. We can be self righteous.
The question we must always hold before us is this: What is the desired outcome? What is the ultimate result of what I, or we, say or do here today? Will these words, this action, serve to tear down, or

build up? Build up self esteem rather than selfish egotism. Build up respect rather than rejection or ridicule. Build up connections rather than walls. Build up care and understanding rather than fear and hatred. Build up hope that little girls and dear old grannies and pigs and wolves and each one of us, wherever we are on our journey, however we tell our stories, can do so with mutual respect, for only then can we begin to know the spirit of the Divine, which dwells within and among us and leads us to true love.